Long Roads, Short Distances

Long Roads, Short Distances

Teaching Writing and Writing Teachers

Brenda Miller Power

HEINEMANN
Portsmouth, NH

Heinemann
A division of Reed Elsevier Inc.
361 Hanover Street
Portsmouth, NH 03801-3912
Offices and agents throughout the world

The author and publisher wish to thank those who have generously given permission to reprint borrowed material:

"Weekly Reading Responses" adapted by permission of Linda Rief: *Seeking Diversity: Language Arts with Adolescents* (Heinemann, A division of Reed Elsevier Inc., Portsmouth, NH, 1992).

Library of Congress Cataloging-in-Publication Data

Power, Brenda Miller.
    Long roads, short distances : teaching writing and writing teachers / Brenda Miller Power ; foreword by Ralph Fletcher.
        p.   cm.
    Includes bibliographical references.
    ISBN 0-435-07240-4
    1. English language—Rhetoric—Study and teaching— Theory, etc.   2. English language—Rhetoric—Study and teaching—United States.   3. English language—Composition and exercises—Theory, etc.   4. English teachers—Training of. I. Title.
PE1404.P617   1997
808'.042'07—dc21   97-14455
                                                                                    CIP

Editor: William Varner
Production: J. B. Tranchemontagne
Manufacturing: Louise Richardson
Cover design: Mary Parker
Cover photo: © 1997 David Lokey/Comstock, Inc.

Printed in the United States of America on acid-free paper
00 99 98 97 DA 1 2 3 4 5 6 7 8 9

for Ruth Shagoury Hubbard,
who kept the faith

Contents

Foreword

When my book *Walking Trees* was published I mailed it to everyone I knew. It was my first book, and I felt giddy as a new parent with a new baby. Tom Romano was the first person to write back.

"Congratulations," he wrote. "You have written a book of stub-your-toe staff development. We need more of these."

Huh? Stub-your-toe? At first it was hard to take this as a compliment. But in time I saw that Romano had hit on a crucial aspect of my book. Teaching—especially teaching teachers—isn't always pretty. And it definitely doesn't always go the way we think it ought to go.

Romano's words come back to me as I read *Long Roads, Short Distances: Teaching Writing and Writing Teachers* by Brenda Miller Power. While many writers promise to open up to us about their teaching, I have never read a book that quite does it the way this one does.

Brenda tells her story in the first person. She talks to us. A first-person book like this one works to the extent that readers want to spend time thinking along with the narrator, occupying her consciousness, living with her elation and despair, following her musings, reflections, and epiphanies.

It doesn't take long for us to discover that this is an author we want to go along with. Brenda Power has a supple, wide-ranging mind and, equally important, a sense of humor. She makes her points through stories, memories, observations, students' writing, and a profusion of amazing metaphors that give this book texture and keep us on our toes.

This book describes Brenda's work with preservice students at the University of Maine. Brenda loves to teach, and she wants her teachers-to-be to develop a similar kind of love. She wants them to love the "ordinary dailyness," the small surprises, that teaching entails.

Brenda writes with tremendous respect about the students with whom she works, seeing them as representatives of another culture with its own set of rituals, values, and rites of passage. It is fascinating to observe the various attitudes she takes toward her students—sometimes curious and sympathetic, at other times perplexed and astonished at their antics and their writing.

This book sets forth a wealth of provocative ideas on the teaching of writing. During one class, Brenda demonstrates the need for a more spontaneous, spur-of-the-moment response to writers working on their drafts. Peter Elbow has suggested that a good writing teacher needs to be a "good host and good bouncer," that is, both supportive and demanding. As a teacher Brenda reveals herself in both roles. She is sympathetic to her students' struggles, but she has high standards, too. Professor Power expects her students to write, and she takes this writing seriously. Her students' writing gives us a clear window into their feelings about teaching: excitement, fear, exhaustion, anger at how little respect teaching gets in our society.

I found this book rich, and richly layered. The story begins with the word *methodos*, or journey; there are many journeys in this book, and they have a way of echoing off each other. We watch the journeys of several new teachers: Beth, who is jolted after not getting into a creative writing class she wants to take, or Tammy, who writes a blistering response to one of Brenda's classes.

This book is rich with mentors, those "midwives to our dreams." We read about the mentors who changed Brenda's life, and we are left with no doubt that Brenda's students will be deeply affected by their contact with her.

Finally—and I mean this as the highest compliment of all—this book is rich with failure. I am reminded of the principal who hired a new teacher with the stipulation that she have at least two interesting failures during the year. An invitation like that recognizes that risk taking is not just a nice idea but perhaps the crucial ingredient for professional growth. Brenda's book suggests the same thing. She courageously shows us all her teaching, warts and all. We watch as her preconceived notions of one student prove to be false. And in my favorite chapter, we get several vivid portraits of her most difficult students, who try Brenda's patience almost to the breaking point, who "are never shy about walking through those holes between my theories and my practice."

There is a lot of substance in this slender book. It chronicles numerous breakthroughs in Brenda's teaching as well as the most painful moments. But there are transcendent moments, too. *Long Roads, Short Distances* is, finally, a hopeful book. I see it as an essential survival manual for all of us trying to become the teachers we hope to be.

— Ralph Fletcher

Acknowledgments

My mother, Dolores Miller, was the first person to show me how joyful a life in teaching can be. She is a high school chemistry teacher. I have many memories of how she opened her home and her heart to students. Over the years, these students have kept in touch with her through cards, visits, and phone calls, telling my mother that they became science teachers or chemists or doctors because of her. My ideal has always been to have that same profound influence in helping my students love writing. I am indebted to many people who share my commitment to good writing and good teaching. Like my mother's influence, their imprint on this book runs so deep that it is impossible to give them all their due. But I do need to name at least a few people. Without them, I might still be writing and teaching, but I would never have produced this book.

I thank the folks at Heinemann, especially my editor William Varner. When words were failing me, Bill showed an intuitive sense of what I wanted to say. His chapter notes were at times more thoughtful than the chapters themselves, and his responses always made me eager to return to the draft and improve it. Sandra Wilde and Jean Ann Clyde also were essential coaches in my writing of this book, through the suggestions for revision they gave as reviewers for Heinemann.

I thank the many colleagues who shepherded me as I learned how to work with undergraduates, especially Arlene Sylvester. Arlene is the administrative assistant who helps me and all my University of Maine education colleagues advise undergraduates. She tempers an encyclopedic knowledge of credit requirements with a quiet warmth that lets every student and faculty member know we will figure it out together. Arlene's professionalism lifts us up and provides a safety net.

I thank the many students who have contributed to this text

through their insights and exuberance, especially Amy Hofmann, Cheryl Maroney, and Jennifer Leida. These women were students in my very first undergraduate writing course, and they set me on a path of combining my interests in writing instruction with an understanding of the rituals and routines of student culture. In recent years, Judith Bradshaw Brown, Kelly Chandler, Cindy Hatt and Cindy McCallister were the doctoral students who forced me to articulate my beliefs about teaching more clearly, in order to help them learn to be good college teachers. They are that, and they honor me with the quality of their teaching.

I thank those who are most responsible for helping me build a university career with teaching at the heart of it. Robert Cobb is simply the finest dean of education in the country today. Bob cares most that I keep my family first in my life, but his own career is a testament to how much can be accomplished professionally when you have a passion for making schools better. Walter Harris and Anne Pooler are the associate deans who supervise my teaching daily. My teaching knowledge is revised, extended, and deepened when I have mentors like Walt and Anne who trust my intentions, and who can help me weigh those intentions against the needs of my students when there are differences. Collectively, Bob, Walt, and Anne have almost fifty years of experience in their current roles as deans. I think they thrive on the challenges of leading, because in those fifty years they have not allowed themselves one moment of cynicism about students or the faculty in their care. I can't imagine being evaluated by anyone other than this trio, because I can't imagine anyone valuing my work more.

It's been said that writers don't write for the masses—they write for an audience of one. I believe those words, and the audience of one for this book is Ruth Shagoury Hubbard. Ruth has listened and responded to my teaching blunders and triumphs for thirteen years. I chose her as my mentor because she is the best college teacher I've ever known, and the best friend I will ever know.

Finally, I thank my husband, David, and my daughter, Deanna. They show much patience with my keyboard pecking and head scratching when it comes to trying to write about my students. As I write this, it is five days before Christmas. Today, three-year-old Deanna asked Santa "for another momma, just like the one I've got. So when my momma is working, I'll always have another momma to play with." With the completion of this book, we both get the next best thing— a mom who has much less writing to do and much more time for play.

One

Methods as a Journey

Sometimes you have to travel a long road to come back a short distance.

— Edward Albee, *The Zoo Story*

Look up *method* in the dictionary, and you find this definition: "a means or manner of procedure, especially, a regular and systematic way of accomplishing anything."

I work with methods students at a university, adults who will soon be teachers. What they expect to learn in my writing methods courses are procedures, systems, and plans for helping children become writers. These are what I was taught when I took methods courses fifteen years ago—schemes researched and certified for teaching grammar, for coming up with creative writing exercises, for structuring writing response groups.

I don't teach as I was taught. I learned the hard way that there is no foolproof plan for helping students become literate. Look closely at the definition of *methods*, and you find the root word, *methodos*. The word is Greek, and it means "a going after" or "journey." In place of foolproof plans and definitions, I launch my students on a journey. They go to seek the knowledge of what it means to be a writer—for themselves and for their students. In contrast to methods, a methodos is a kind of personal quest. Each student finds his or her own way, with my help and the help of peers. Only then will methods emerge that make sense to students, that they understand well enough to apply in their own class-rooms someday.

This book is the story of some long roads traveled with students that always lead back a short distance—to how I am still learning to teach through the daily lessons my students give me. For years now, the books that have spoken to my students most eloquently are not filled with recipes for success but with stories of real teachers in real classrooms. Nancie Atwell, Jane Doan and Penny Chase, Patricia McLure, Linda Rief, Donald Murray—all have opened their classrooms and lives up for eloquent examination and reflection. Their stories have endured through the teaching of my students. These teachers don't divorce their teaching from their lives, and so their classrooms come to life.

There is a curious absence of books written about college-level methods teaching with a personal and critical tone. This is my attempt to write the book I would like to read—the story of one teacher learning to work with future elementary writing teachers. It is a story filled with bumps in the road, forays into the ditch, and wrong turns. But it is also the story of learning to pull over and rethink the destination, of turning the wheel over to students, of enjoying the detours that ended up being the best part of the trip. It is my story, and it is still very much a journey in progress.

My Teaching Methodos

My own journey of learning to teach has some painful roots. It begins with the first writing class I ever taught, freshman composition at a community college. I was enrolled in a master's degree program at the time at a large midwestern university. An opportunity popped up to teach two freshman composition courses during the winter semester at a community college forty-five minutes away. Armed with knowledge of the writing process, high-quality writing exercises, and a will to succeed, I knew I would enjoy what I learned from these students.

Teaching those two classes was the most miserable experience of my life. Often at least one third of my students were absent. Only a handful of those who did attend even tried to complete any reading or writing assignments between class sessions. Many were functionally illiterate, writing at a third-grade level.

I frantically searched the literature for exercises and activities that would reach these students. In the first weeks, I was optimistic almost every time I walked into the classroom. I had mantras I would say in the car during my commute—this would be the day, this would be the activity, this would be our moment of breakthrough.

I was always wrong. Every suggestion I made was met with blank stares, and students continually reminded me the only reason they took the class was because it was required. They didn't want to be there, and I soon dreaded my time with them.

Being only a few years older than my students didn't help. I would dress in drab brown wool skirts and blazers, pull my hair into a tight bun, and put heavy concealer over any acne outbreaks. I hoped this would make me look older and wiser. Instead, it usually just made me look very young and very dowdy.

Good mornings were the ones on which my students and I made an unspoken pact to engage in what Ted Sizer (1984, 156) calls "the conspiracy of the Least." I would go through a lesson in a desultory fashion, students would scribble something in their notebooks, and the hour would pass mercifully fast. It was the least effort any of us could manage, a tick above breathing or sleeping in output of energy.

Bad mornings were the ones that began with me standing by the car, in the pitch-black of a frigid Michigan morning, trying unsuccessfully to get my key into the frozen door lock. I would return to the house, root around for an extension cord and hair-dryer, and blow-dry the lock open. I would drive hard and still arrive minutes late to teach.

There were mornings like this when it just wasn't possible

3

to go through with our conspiracy, when I would do the task I dreaded most—circulating among my students for individual conferences.

On one morning, I sat facing Stephen. Stephen was working on his "I-Search" paper (Macrorie 1980). This was one of those writing assignments that were guaranteed to succeed. Students picked their own research topic and then had lots of time to go out into the world and find answers to their research questions. Stephen's topic was his future as an engineer. He had dreams of traveling the same road I did, to the big university forty-five minutes away, after he finished his associate's degree.

I had visions of students like Stephen interviewing engineers, spending a day at an engineering firm to get a feel for the work, and surveying engineering students at the university who were finishing their degrees and could talk about the quality of the program.

Stephen had visions of me that morning complimenting him on his four-sentence final draft of his paper, with all the information in it culled from a thirty-year-old textbook on careers in technical fields that he had found down the hall in the eight shelves of books that served as the school library.

In our conference, I suggested he talk to engineers or get some resource materials from the university as a way of "fleshing out" that final draft. Stephen was silent, slumping ever lower in his chair. Finally, he blurted out, "Do I have to?" I responded, "Don't you want to know these things?" He shot back, "Let's cut to the chase. Will this affect my grade?"

I paused then, as I often do when it's best not to blurt out the first thing that pops into my head. What I wanted to say was, "No, Stephen, it won't affect your grade, but it will affect your life. You and your cronies in this class all have big plans to be doctors or lawyers or engineers because you want to make lots of money. You want to get out of this town. But I hear you talk. I know you're flunking chemistry, I know you're flunking math, and you surely can't think you're going to pass this course. I know you're going to college as a weak second choice after losing hope of landing a union job in the plants. Do you think marking time at this place is going to make you an engineer?"

I knew Stephen and his friends came from families who had worked for the past three generations in the local automobile parts factories. These were high-paying jobs and represented the only way of life these families had ever known. But all these plants had closed or cut back production in the time Stephen and his friends had passed through the public schools.

And so they were here, the first generation from their families to go to college. They didn't have a clue about the differences between high school and college expectations, about how life as an engineer or lawyer might be different from life as a factory worker. And I didn't have a clue how to help them use literacy to understand those differences.

It was a long pause in that conference. During that pause, all those words in that wonderful speech in the bubble above my head just faded away. Finally, I said quietly, "Yes. If you don't do more, it will affect your grade."

I looked down the row of students. Maybe the next one would offer some relief or insight. But my next conference was with a young man who had been sending me mash notes every week. I'd referred him to the counseling center and for remedial skills testing. His remedial skills report came back— he was borderline mentally retarded. I was thankful I wasn't going to receive a report from the counseling center. His thick black glasses were held together with masking tape. He gave me a crooked smile. At least one of us was looking forward to our one-on-one time.

To say I had the desire to flee that classroom by running out the door would be an understatement. In that moment I looked out the window longingly at the concrete plaza three stories below. Surely the impact of the fall could be no worse than how devastating these students were to my concepts of what writing instruction should be.

When I left that place each day, I would drive as fast as I

could. The college was one of those gray concrete monoliths that rises out of the bare expanse of a former cornfield. And that's what it was for me, too—a massive ugly lump on the smooth landscape of what I had mapped out as my professional future.

I would drive away from the college, past the rusting factories, past the neat tract homes where these students lived with their parents. It was a lonely drive. I had never before experienced serious failure. The problems here were deep-rooted and complex, going beyond student distaste for writing. I wasn't equipped to deal with them.

When I entered the classroom and heard heavy sighs as I asked students to write, I tried to put on a teacher's mind. I willed myself to dredge up every ounce of intuition and common sense I had. Good teachers must have some way to break through these barriers, I thought. Putting on that teacher's mind felt like I was strapping onto my head a tin can that contained a lone dried pea. Not much seemed to be rattling around up there as I searched for solutions to classroom problems.

It should have been the best possible time of learning for me. I was in a fine graduate program. I brought my problems every afternoon to seminar classes. Most of the other students were teachers. But books and professors weren't much help. Suggested techniques and exercises guaranteed to succeed didn't seem to reach these students. After a while, I just quit sharing my problems. I knew I was being perceived as a quitter and a complainer. I was too embarrassed to admit the depth of my problems with those students and my inability to make these "foolproof" methods work.

I began to believe in the concept of the born teacher. Others in the same position were succeeding with these kinds of students. I decided some people must be born knowing how to deal with all those individual faces and histories, with the unexpected twists in the best-laid plans. I imagined those teachers' minds were rich banquets of strategies, special insights, and common sense. And what had God given me? A lone dried pea. Perhaps, instead of being a born teacher, I was one of those born whiners who mark time in so many teachers' lounges—complaining bitterly about the lack of respect and effort from students over steaming mugs of coffee, animated only in those moments daily when they discuss the new Avon or Amway products they sell on the side to make ends meet.

I moved on to doctoral work at the University of New Hampshire. After my dismal start in teaching, dealing with students and literacy as an abstraction seemed a safe escape from full-time teaching. But from the first days in the program, I was sent into public elementary classrooms throughout the area to observe, research, and learn. I'm glad now that there was no escape from real teachers and students.

I knew I wanted to work with adult learners. One of the quick side trips I made in those first weeks of the program was into Patricia McLure's first-grade classroom at Mast Way School in Lee, New Hampshire. I planned to stay a few days, find out everything I needed to know about primary literacy instruction, and leave. I finally left three years later, doctorate in hand. After three years, I had learned that there was so much more I wanted to learn about young readers and writers.

I remember my second day in Pat's class. Students were filing out for morning recess. I held in my hands a piece of writing by a girl in the class. I asked Pat if I could have a copy of the writing—it was adorable. Pat said, "I don't know. You'll have to ask Stacey when she comes in from recess." I was floored. I'd read about respect for learners, but wasn't this carrying things a bit too far? Pat made me ask kids for permission for *everything*. Who was in charge here, anyway?!

What I learned from Pat in those first hours in her classroom was to respect students so deeply that you gave them as much control as possible over their learning. I thought about how I liked to be treated as an adult, and I saw Pat give children the same degree of attention and concern. When I worked with Pat, I wondered how different my first teaching experience would have been if even once I had pulled over to the side of the road on my way home from teaching and knocked on the doors of a few of those tract homes instead of just driving by as fast as I could. I realized from Pat that teaching was a lot more complicated and messy and wonderful than I had thought.

I became hopeful in Pat's room. Maybe if the Stephens of the world had spent a few years with the Pat McLures of the world before they met me, they would have been ready to learn. I began to think about working with elementary teachers and teaching them what I had learned from Pat.

I saw Pat sit with students in conferences, carefully and thoughtfully encouraging those youngsters. Here was great teaching, the role model I sought. And plenty of what I saw could be imitated and filed away for future use. I began to believe the principles she was using could work at any age level.

The tin can began to fill. I began to talk like Pat—my speech became slower, more measured. She tackled classroom problems every day, and I took notes. As I began to teach adults again later that year, all practicing elementary teachers, I thought of Pat when problems came up. How would Pat approach this presentation? this assignment? I asked for advice, and she gave it. I was growing up, finally developing a teacher's mind, and it belonged to Pat McLure. I even began to prefer her brands of herb teas and coffee.

And then I was assigned to another first-grade classroom my second year of graduate school. Chris Gaudet, of Stratham Memorial School, was as gregarious as Pat was reserved. I decided that Chris must be doing things wrong. She worked from the same set of principles as Pat, based upon the same theorists and teachers as Pat, but her classroom was so different. While Pat had quiet chats with students, Chris had boisterous improvisations of storybook characters.

But within weeks, I knew that Chris was also a great teacher. This posed a dilemma in my developing teacher's mind. I could resolve it only by accepting that there was more than one solution to problems that came up in the classroom.

That tin can began to fill with more possibilities, and I found I had more than one way of dealing with situations. I even found that I would do some things differently than Pat, Chris, or the other teachers I met. Every fine teacher I met at the university and in the schools offered more possibilities for instruction. I continue to meet teachers who offer more solutions to the same problems.

What these teachers have in common is that they don't work in isolation. They know who their role models as teachers are, even if some of these models are teachers and theorists they know only through research and articles. They enjoy learning what solutions other teachers have found, and meeting teachers on and off the page who have grappled with similar problems. And even though they may tackle some of the same problems differently, their belief systems and theories of learning are often remarkably alike.

When I think of that part of me that is always thinking about what it means to teach and how I can improve as a teacher, I no longer see a tin can. My image is that of a great stage. Mekeel McBride (1985) puts forth this image in her reflections on the writer's brain:

> I think there's some part of a writer's brain or an artist's brain that is always working on the poem or the painting. You might not have access to it because there are big phone bills to pay and there's hurricane Gloria and classes to be taught and sick pets and so on. But I envision this part of my brain that's like a giant Hollywood prop set where everything exists. Where I could find, if I needed to, Cleopatra's shoe size. I could find out how the wolverine feels about snowmobiles. I think that everything is occurring in this part of my brain. I think that the minute I get inspiration for a poem, the prop people get it all figured out and set up and it's there. The business of sitting down to write, and going through draft after draft, is a way of getting to that vision that's already complete somewhere in my brain. And even if that isn't a true vision, it's really comforting.

I believe some part of my mind is always working on improving my teaching. My teacher's mind doesn't contain lots of props. Instead, it has lots of teachers in the wings, ready to improvise as I present problems to be acted out on that stage. A student asks a sticky question in a conference? I call Nancie Atwell on stage and envision how she might handle that student. Then I might bring out Pat McLure, for a different perspective on the same issue. If I have trouble with an administrator, Susan Ohanian is brought out from the wings. She has the right combination of guts and humor to deal with bureaucracy. When I'm frustrated at the choices a student is making, I bring out Jane Doan and Penny Chase. They always have more patience than I do with understanding and honoring student choices.

I've read about and seen teachers dealing with students who have no desire to write, and yet these teachers get the job done. I've seen teachers teach in the midst of countless intercom interruptions, and comfort students who bring severe problems from home into the classroom. I laughed when Susan Ohanian wrote of a cockroach appearing under her desk when she was trying to teach. And then the largest roach I've ever seen appeared in the middle of a challenging conference I was having with a student three months later.

I do get bogged down with schedules, time constraints, and bureaucratic needs that sometimes keep me away from improving myself through using that stage. That's part of any teacher's life. But it's a comfort for me to know it is there. I know that everything I've experienced as a teacher that challenges the principles I try to carry out in my classroom has been experienced by others before me. I can turn to them for support and solutions.

I have dozens of teachers—people I've met in classrooms, heard at conferences, or read about in articles that present their classrooms and research—whom I carry with me. The work of these teachers is principled and theory-driven. It's not that the methods and principles I was trying to apply in that first teaching job weren't true. But they were skeletons. The five-step or eight-step writing process teaching plan couldn't help me with the complex and difficult day-to-day interactions that are teaching. Incidents from classrooms where a child-centered curriculum comes to life put flesh and bone on the theories.

The Methodos of Students

My students come to me unsure of themselves as teachers. It's not hard for me to step into their shoes. I know many ponder the question of whether they are "born teachers." Some know they were born *wanting* to teach, but they don't know if they have the ability to be good teachers. They expect to learn five- and seven-step plans in my class, foolproof schemes for helping children become literate. They want to know what it takes to be the best. They want to know if they will be good teachers. I don't give them what they expect. But I hope I give them what they need.

If a student asked me if she had what it took to be a great teacher, I wouldn't ask her if she loved kids. Working hard is important, but I wouldn't ask about her commitment, either, or about her public-speaking abilities. I would ask, Do you like classroom incidents? Do you like looking closely at what goes on, minute by minute, in a classroom that works? Is it a pleasure for you to read about and observe fine teachers inspiring children's minds? Great teachers like seeing other great teachers in action. They look for models, for others more experienced in specific tasks, in order to help themselves tackle those tasks. It's a lifelong search, and in the end the work of such teachers endures through the lives of students they've touched.

When I start my students on their methodos, their journeys into writing instruction, I have to help them get inside some of these model teachers' classrooms. They will meet them in articles, on videotapes, and in local public schools. They need to start a conversation with these teachers and their peers, even if it's just voices in their minds or enactments on their own stages of different possibilities for classrooms. I need to help them realize that the best teachers aren't on the journey alone. Only then will the techniques and theories of current literacy instruction come to life.

We take time together to see multiple possibilities for the classroom. I want my students to learn that often mistakes will be their best teachers. The activities that fail, or learners who disrupt the class, are the best teachers for future teachers—as long as you have interested colleagues who can help you sort through what went wrong and why.

It is hard to learn to teach, but I believe for most of my students the experience is what Donald Murray would call "hard fun." They aren't sure where their journeys will lead, but they aren't venturing out alone, either. This book is the story of some of the roads students take as they come to know their own role models. It's the story of how they learn to see classrooms and themselves in new ways as they read and write. And it's a very personal story of my own struggles in trying to figure out my role in the classroom.

Tubas and Burning Houses: The State of Teacher Education

I can't look at my journey of learning to teach writing, or at the journeys of my students, without briefly considering recent twists and turns in the path of teacher education. I don't work in a vacuum. The way future teachers are taught in this country is under attack from many different fronts.

Educators are always being put on the defensive in our society for what we know and do. One of the problems is that our job looks simple, as Susan Ohanian (1991, 332) writes:

> What we do looks fairly easy; most people feel they could do the teaching part, though they acknowledge that putting up with the kids all day might be a bit difficult.

Everyone in our society has spent years in classrooms, and education is a public enterprise. People feel that they know from experience quite a bit about life in schools and that they have a right to be critical. All levels of education come under attack in our society. But specific groups of educators seem to bear the brunt of the criticism at different times.

For most of the past few decades, high school teachers have been condemned for producing too many students who can't read or write. Surveys are conducted revealing that a small percentage of high schoolers think Adolf Hitler was a game show host or that Cuba is near Antarctica. This frightens parents and employers, and they demand to know what is being taught in schools. They also demand change.

Lately there has been a not-so-subtle shift in criticism toward college instruction. New surveys show how little college juniors and seniors know about geography, math, and literature. There are calls for a comprehensive college curriculum with testing and standards set throughout the country.

If college instruction in general is beginning to receive strong criticism, teacher education specifically has been on the hot seat for a few years. Alternative plans for preparing teachers that eliminate the education major and drastically reduce required education courses have been developed in a number of states. Three state legislatures (California, Texas, and Virginia) mandated in the late 1980s that the education major be eliminated in all their state higher education institutions. Many government officials echo the views of the general public when they describe education courses as worthless. The leader of the drive for reform in Texas, State Senator Carl Parker, has this to say about colleges of education (Watts 1989, 312):

> I believe colleges of education [are] abusing teacher preparation programs by including redundant material in their courses, substituting education courses for courses in other fields, and requiring worthless content. . . . That's ridiculous. We [want] to force colleges of education to reexamine their curricula—to include the essentials and cut the crap.

That's pretty blunt, isn't it? It isn't often that you hear a public figure use the words *abuse* and *crap*, particularly with reference to teacher preparation programs. Our profession has responded in recent years to these biting attacks and urgent calls for reform with the "outcomes and standards" movement. It seems like all the professional organizations I'm involved in, and many others, are investing an enormous amount of energy trying to come up with statements that explain what we're trying to do in a pithy way. The idea is that these outcomes or standards will be the proof that what we do has value. The hope is that these standards will lead to something that can be measured, weighed, or at least verified through systematic observation and assessment.

I know these organizations mean well, and I respect how hard my colleagues are working to come up with standards and outcomes. But whenever I sift through the cumbersome documents they send me filled with numbered statements and jargon du jour, I get a strange sensation. I feel like I'm sitting in the ruins of a fortune cookie factory that has just exploded. All the same words flutter around, words like *competency*, and *risk taking*, and *independence*. I don't think we'll ever capture the complexity and magic of what fine teachers do through a series of outcomes or a carefully explicated set of standards.

And that's the challenge for all teachers—recreating what we really do for others. It's so much easier to try to find something, anything, to quantify. But that doesn't begin to capture what really goes on in good teaching. I think what Steinbeck (1941, 264) said about a fish applies also to teaching:

> The Mexican Sierra has 17 plus 15 plus 9 spines in the dorsal fin. These can be easily counted. But if the Sierra strikes hard on the line so that our hands are burned, if the fish sounds and nearly escapes and finally comes in over the rail, his colors pulsing and his tail beating the air, a whole new relational externality has come into being—an entity which is more than the sum of the fish plus the fisherman. The only way to count the spines of the Sierra unaffected by this second relational reality is to sit in a laboratory, open an evil-smelling jar, remove a still colorless fish

from the formaldehyde solution, count the spines, and write the truth. . . . There you have recorded a reality which cannot be assailed—probably the least important reality concerning the fish or yourself.

Too much of what's written about working with future writing teachers are those "least important realities"—the truths that can be measured from surveying large numbers of beginning teachers. The same can be said for most of the standards and outcomes statements I've read. I wouldn't disagree with most of the statements in these reports—there is truth in them. But they really don't explain what I do, either. The most important truths for me have emerged from the lives and stories of my students, and the lives of writing teachers who have taught me their craft. It's been a long and idiosyncratic road back a short distance to some simple truths—that teaching must begin with the lives of the students, that teachers must be writers themselves, that all my growth as a teacher is rooted in my ability to stay fresh as a learner.

State legislators might have little patience with talk of writing methods as a journey, with my acknowledgment and support of different students learning different things in my courses. They might not share my belief that writing instruction doesn't begin with foolproof schemes and formulas, but with the teacher's own literacy. But I also believe folks like Senator Parker and the many others who castigate teachers at all levels will probably go to their graves with the firm suspicion that all we do in elementary methods courses is show our students 101 different uses for a felt board.

What follows, individual stories of the roads my students and I have taken in our journey to understand how to teach writing, may seem inappropriate given the nature of debates about literacy and the expressed need of so many to standardize what is taught and learned at all levels. But I hope explanations of my students' beliefs, learning processes, and experiences in schools can provide some insights for reexamining critical issues in teacher education. Like many reformers at the state and federal levels, I want dramatic changes in programs for teachers. But my image of a well-prepared teacher may be far different from theirs.

When I write these words, I feel like the poet of whom Tess Gallagher (1985, 114) writes:

> The poet is like a tuba player in a house on fire. Crucial events surround him, threatening to devour, while he makes inappropriate music with an instrument that cannot help causing its serious manipulator to look ridiculous.

The burning house may be the state of teacher education programs today. I don't have a lot of control over the future of methods courses or teacher preparation programs. And at a time when education departments are losing control of requirements for future teachers, it may be absurd to argue for less control of content presented in methods courses. Instead of putting water on the flames, I'm choosing to play the tuba. My song may seem ridiculous.

But I don't know any other way to begin to solve some of the deep, systemic problems in public schools today. I've come far enough in understanding how little I know to realize there are no easy solutions for these complex problems. What teachers do only looks easy. Eliminating teacher preparation programs is an acceptance of that surface view of teaching as an activity any well-meaning person off the street could handle.

I don't believe that, and neither does anyone who's spent more than a few hours recently in a typical public elementary school. I want my students to begin to solve some of the problems in these schools, to close some of the gaps between theory and practice. This is a lot to expect from young adults, and it won't happen unless I apply the principles I teach.

Perhaps the most important principle I want them to accept is the belief that their students are competent and knowledgeable. The students they work with will bring different cultures and concerns into the classroom that have to be acknowledged and incorporated into the writing curriculum.

My first responsibility as a methods instructor is to acknowledge that I'm not teaching writing methods—I'm working with *writers*, students with histories. And I must put a structure in place that can tap into those life histories.

Two

Between Worlds:
The Lives of Future Teachers

*My imagination takes its strength and guides its direction from
what I see and hear and learn and feel and remember of my
living world. But I was to learn slowly that both these worlds,
outer and inner, were different from what they seemed to me in
the beginning.*

— Eudora Welty, *One Writer's Beginnings*

Change is slow, difficult, hard to see or gauge.
Sometimes. Maybe. Perhaps. But not always. Change can also
be rapid, awkward, and intense. There are times when you
can predict or expect tremendous change in students. Teachers recognize this. Ask teachers what grades they prefer to
teach, and you will find out where rapid change takes place. I
have students soon to be teachers who tell me, "I'll teach
kindergarten or second grade, but not first grade. You have to
help them crack the reading code. They learn too much too
quickly. It's too much responsibility." Some teachers are eager
to work with students undergoing tremendous change, and
others prefer ages of slow growth.

Change can be frightening for a teacher. There is no age
group that spooks teachers more than junior high. I used to
believe that Nancie Atwell's book *In the Middle* (1987) was a
remarkable chronicle of adolescent literacy. It is, but I now
see it as much more than that. Atwell captures students

changing. When change is rapid, it is marked by moments of insight and transition. When I read her book, I see young teens talking smart while they clutch teddy bears to their chests. These students are between child and adult worlds, and Atwell respects this as she documents it.

When I read *In the Middle*, I think about how much better college life would be if we took Atwell's approach. In one of my favorite research studies, *Coming of Age in New Jersey* (Moffatt 1990), an anthropology professor from New Jersey felt like he was losing touch with students. In order to understand their culture, he did a research study where he lived in a dorm for one day and night a week. It's an amazing book. So much of what we do in and out of classrooms on campus is based upon what we *think* students need. But we're basing it on our culture, not necessarily on our students' lives, needs, and interests. No wonder attendance at so many carefully planned campus functions is poor.

When you change your mind-set to view your students as another culture, whether you're working with first graders, adolescents, or a university methods class, the group becomes fascinating. What are their rituals? their rites of passage? the key values in the group? These are the same questions broached by an anthropologist in a grass hut, far from home.

But when you don't view your students as a separate culture, you're inevitably disappointed. You see them as smaller, lesser versions of your own culture. I think this is why Atwell's book has had such an enormous impact in schools. She was the first to show the uniqueness of "in the middlers." They aren't hormone-charged elementary students, they aren't high school wannabes. They have unique traits that need to be respected, if only because they will soon outgrow them.

Many of my students are also between worlds during their junior and senior years of college. They will soon be leaving the teen years and sheltered college life for the teaching profession. They are beginning to spend extended time in public schools, getting their first taste of what teaching will be like. I want to try to document some of the changes my students go through, some of the tensions they feel as they prepare for their own classrooms. Much of the change takes place in their minds, as they adjust from thoughts of being a student to images of being a teacher.

It's a metamorphosis. The clichéd image of the metamorphosis of a caterpillar becoming a butterfly. There are two stages in this transformation that get the least emphasis. The cocoon doesn't play well, because there isn't much to see. Teachers who work with students who are rapidly changing can get frustrated, because students can keep a lot of their thoughts and feelings inside during this time. Young children, adolescents, and young adults will sometimes only give you brief glimpses into their hearts and minds as they change. The changes can be overwhelming, and many students don't realize their peers are going through similar experiences.

The other stage is the pupa, just before the adult butterfly emerges. The pupa is wet, unformed, unattractive. The period of final drying out and transformation is hard and awkward. It's not easy to watch, but at the same time it's fascinating.

A professor working with students who will soon teach gets glimpses of all stages of the metamorphosis. What I've learned to expect are tensions and extremes. A student in an expensive suit sits next to a student in torn blue jeans. One worked in the public schools that day; the other slept in and did her homework while watching soap operas before our afternoon class.

A word spoken to one of my students with a sliver too little tact can easily bring an outburst of tears. At the same time, the smallest kindnesses can bring hugs and cries of happiness. Teaching is often an intense experience. Working with students who are eager, unsure, and changing heightens that intensity.

Defining what students know and believe, and who they are as they are beginning to teach, can be as elusive as pinning down a butterfly. And my goal isn't to pin them against the wall, but to get a glimpse of their first flights as teachers.

I remember sitting in my office, reading a student journal during my first year of working with undergraduates. A student was writing about her educational philosophy. She dissected the work of Piaget, Bloom, and Vygotsky with precision. I turned the page, anticipating some more remarkable insights from this young woman. The next journal entry was about her twenty-first birthday that week and about how she became so drunk that she had to lie down on the sidewalk in the middle of town at 3 a.m. before going home that night. She wrote that she had never had that much fun in her life. Then she remembered that the entries were supposed to in some way refer to her future as a teacher, so she added, "I guess what I want to say is that I want my students to have fun. But not fun like that, of course. Oh, my head is still fuzzy. Bye." So much for Piaget.

The image of public drunkenness isn't too amusing. But as I flipped back and forth between those journal entries, I had to shake my head in amazement at the worlds this woman was moving between. My students enjoy taking on adult responsibilities, putting forth their views, and taking stands. At the same time, they've finally gotten the teen scene down and aren't eager to leave it behind.

I can be astonished at my students' dependence on me, their parents, and others for decisions. I sometimes see them in the cocoon, unwilling or unable to take the initiative in their learning. One term I assigned only the first three sections of a book. The text had five major sections. A student wrote in her journal about how much she had enjoyed the book:

> This is not even like reading a book! I learned so much that I can't wait to turn the pages and see what will come next. I think it is the best book I've ever read. Do you think you might assign the last part of the book? I would really like to read it, so I hope you change your mind and do, so I can.

I didn't change my mind and assign more of the book. I tried to imagine a book I'd found delightful, the best book I'd ever read, sitting on my bedstand. Then I cut to the vision of my-self sitting in bed, waiting for someone, my college professor, to tell me I had to read it before I could pick it up and finish it. I don't know if that student ever did finish the book.

And just when I begin to believe that my students are pas-sive and unmotivated, I get a glimpse of how much energy they will throw into projects that they believe in. Staying up all night to work is a way of life for them, an existence they don't realize will soon pass. Because they don't yet have many of the adult commitments of running households and fami-lies, they can put their hearts into projects and commitments with an energy that astonishes. This is also the time when they are coming out of the cocoon, and taking on responsibil-ity is a delight for them. Jenny captures that zest in her short passage about working on an art project:

> I love solitude. I'll never forget putting in three or four hours at the art room frosh year. It was about 3:30 a.m. and I wasn't fin-ished with my project, but I felt so good about it I left for home. I rode my bike down Main Street the opposite way of traffic, and behind me came an eighteen-wheeler going down Main Street the wrong way like me. I loved it. I felt so good. I was singing and I wanted it to rain so I could be feeling even more alive.

It's exhilarating to read Jenny's words. I'm past the age when I might race with that truck.

A small percentage of students I work with are middle-aged, returning to school for certification after having had children or pursuing other career options. This minority plays an important role in challenging the views of the younger students, as the rest of this book will reveal. These older students have the same concerns I do in their personal lives—finding good child care, juggling school with family re-sponsibilities. But most of my methods students are just leav-ing their teen years, and this is the culture I spend most of my time trying to understand.

I've identified three common points of conflict for most of the students I work with. My students struggle with the public's and their own perceptions of teaching. They will soon leave home, and they are reexamining their relationships with family and friends. They actively seek role models for teaching, and at the same time, are often harshly critical of the teachers they see around them. These conflicts put them between worlds. They have carried inside of them vague, ideal visions of what they will be like as teachers for some time. Sometimes this vision changes and is challenged by the realities of the teaching life—the outside world they are exploring in new ways.

I don't completely understand these conflicts, how my students work through them, or how they manage to stay on their feet in different worlds. I'm learning to accept that it may never be possible to fully understand students who are changing, but I've learned to respect and enjoy watching the process.

R-E-S-P-E-C-T

Respect is the most important issue my students deal with. They move between feeling pride about their career choice and embarrassment at the public's perceptions of teachers. As my students envision themselves as teachers, they become more aware of the public's perception of teaching. Jake contrasted his history of respect for teachers with the current perception of the profession:

> When I was younger I worshipped my teachers. I respected and looked up to them. They were authority figures and I never thought of crossing that line of authority. But these days it seems different. Since I've been going to the university, I sense a very different opinion of the teaching profession. It seems that a lot of people hadn't held that respect which I had when I was younger. Sometimes I think the only people that respect and support the teaching profession are those in the profession itself.

Students notice relatives' responses to their career plans at parties. I read a lot in journals about angry fathers who encourage their daughters to explore other career options. The full impact of the lack of respect for teaching is tough for some students to handle. Even small public exchanges with strangers can bring harsh insights to my students.

Hannah wanted to buy a new car. She saw the salesman's attitude change before her eyes when she announced her career choice:

> I shouldn't have told the guy I was studying to be a teacher. He tried to sell me the cheapest car on the lot. I don't know where he got the idea that a teacher couldn't have a sporty little car or a car that wasn't ten years old. I finally left the dealership with a new car, but I don't think I left the salesman with a changed image of teachers as a whole.
>
> I only hear two things when I tell people I'm going to be a teacher: (1) It will be nice to have your summers off, or (2) Too bad, it doesn't pay well.
>
> In my opinion, these are two of the worst reasons for getting any job. A person should select an occupation that they will enjoy and excel at.
>
> Human sacrifices are against the law. Yet this country sacrifices its children's intellect and growth by allowing people who would love to teach, or who do love to teach, to get away because the pay and respect are near zero.

Elementary education majors find they don't need to venture off campus to see how little respect their major receives. Many students note how disdainful their friends are of their career choice. Peers in other fields don't believe the education major is much work, as Sarah notes:

> Is the Education College the joke around campus these days? I am beginning to think so. If I had a nickel for every comment about how easy classes must be that I have heard the past three years, I wouldn't be working an extra job. My friend Dave had the nerve to ask me the other day if the Education Resource Center was the place for storing the toys and games we must be using in our classes. Dave, who is a plant science major, got the reply, "Oh, and does it take four years to learn how to water a plant?"

One student with a dual major in education and history noted her professors' responses:

> As soon as one of my history professors knows that I'm also an elementary education major [she] tends to think less of me—or expect less or not take me seriously in general. What is it about being a teacher—an *elementary* school teacher—that makes some people think that you are less of an intellectual? Is it because a lot of *women* go into the profession? So many times when I have heard a crack from a professor or anyone else about how anti-intellectual teachers are, I'd like to say, "If it weren't for a teacher, you would not be where you are, with a Ph.D."

Reading entries like these makes me expect students to be the greatest defenders of the teaching profession and their career choice. Sometimes they are, but they also fear they may turn out like the teachers they dislike. Their vision of the future is sometimes shaped by the past, and these negative images of the future reveal much about their experiences as students:

> Right now I am very confused about what I want to do or be. I am very scared about only being able to do one thing—only being trained to teach. I'm scared about turning into a sadistic wench who wears out-of-date clothes and picks on kids. I would be *so* disappointed. But I want to teach. I love kids. I can't remember not wanting to teach.

Yet most of my students have picked the profession because they believe it is like no other, and they will be doing the most important work there is, as this student writes:

> I'm so glad I'm entering a profession where I can make a difference. There seem to be so many jobs in the world in which everyone is a mere link in the chain, but teaching is different. . . . I hope that one day I can really make a profound difference in a student's life.

These future teachers support and need each other. They spend much time talking about teaching through the many required education courses they take together. But our education building has lots of concrete and few windows, and the air can be stifling. Frankly, sometimes the students get on each others' nerves.

Some see problems in their peers' attitudes. Becky tired of what she termed the "milk and cookies" idealism of her peers. Many of her friends loved Robert Fulghum's essay *All I Ever Needed to Know I Learned in Kindergarten* (1988). In this essay, Fulghum argues for a simpler way of looking at the world and living. Becky found the ideas in the essay mindless, and she often wrote about feeling alienated from her peers because of her views:

> You know what annoys me? When people take time out of class to argue with the teacher over one stupid question on a test that they could have gotten if they would have studied. I think that I will have my students discuss any questions they might have for me on a one-to-one basis. I mean, do these people know how stupid they look? God, that's annoying.
>
> Sometimes I don't know if I should really be a teacher. I mean, I cannot go out there in "La La Land." . . . Sometimes we have to face the cold hard facts—some children will not have parents who care, others have parents who care too much—some children you may not be able to help although you should do everything to help them. I just can't get into the "everyone should have milk and cookies at 3 p.m." view of the world. Sure, it would be nice—but we have to grow up and realize that some days we won't be able to have our milk and our cookies, and the world will still go around.

These future teachers have the option of seeing events through the lens of a student or a teacher, and sometimes the difference in perspectives causes conflicts. During one semester I taught the writing methods course, and a colleague taught the same class in the reading methods course. The students became hostile about a midterm assignment for the reading course, and many chose to write about it in their journals for my class. The students seemed to be evenly divided. Half placed themselves firmly in the world of the student and were furious at the length of the assignment. The other half, including students like Maureen, saw themselves as teachers. They were angry at their peers' response:

> I feel really bad that we got Dr. Jones so mad that she literally yelled at us, in a voice of definite frustration. Some of the students in our section make me angry also. The assignment isn't too much. We are college juniors and seniors, and I don't see any reason why we should be complaining. . . . I was so frustrated at some of the "babies" in our class. Don't get me wrong, I have a lot of work to do, and the thought of writing a seventeen-page midterm doesn't thrill me, but I can deal with it. I wonder how some of my fellow classmates will make it in the real world. . . . Life is not always a bowl of cherries and sometimes we must work hard. What are some people going to do when the principal says I want this, I want that. . . . Do you know what I mean? Some people like to whine and fight until they get what they want.

But even stronger than these occasional annoyances is the bond that students form with their friends. These future teachers support and need each other. By the end of the semester, most are sentimental about these bonds they have formed:

> Last night, another long night talking about teaching with all my roommates who will soon teach. I can't help but think about how soon we will be out there, but I don't feel ready to leave them yet. When I begin to student-teach, who will I find who will listen as well as these people to every little incident from my day?

Allison captures the feelings of many of her peers in her final piece of writing for the class:

> I've gained a lot of respect for my classmates, their ideas, and their commitment. I only wish we could all teach together after graduation instead of separating. Perhaps I'm wrong, but I don't think I'll ever establish the same tie I have with these people. My fellow teachers after graduation won't have the same basis for the bond that all of us share. We've been through the fire together; four years of worries and losses, triumphs and highs, papers and exams, deadlines and all-nighters. I already miss them.

Heroes on and off Pedestals

As my students realize they will soon teach, they become anxious for teachers to emulate. Some of the teachers they read about are placed on pedestals. And at the same time, they save some of their harshest criticism for the teachers they work with who don't fit their vision of good teaching. As the Nancie Atwells rise in stature, professors within the college often take it on the chin:

> Well, I just came from my geology class, and I guess this guy is the perfect teacher for it. Every class he does a great imitation of a *rock*. Don't any of these professors who drone on in a monotone have any clue of how boring they are? I hope I'm at least *slightly* more in touch with my students when I teach. Talk about zero rapport.

As students learn about high-quality teaching, they demand more from the professors they work with:

> The more I read about all the excellent examples of teaching and all these techniques that are being used in more and more classrooms, the more I wish professors at the university level had to continue to take professional development classes not only in their subject area, but also in education. Everyone says that we are now responsible for our own learning, which is true to an extent, but I think that professors have a responsibility to our learning as well. . . . I took a class once where sixty percent either fail or receive a D, and then need to repeat the class. This happens every year. Even people repeating the class have a high percentage of failure. At this point someone needs to look at how that teacher is teaching, because with that many people failing it can't all be the students' fault.

These criticisms of some of my colleagues at the university are certainly valid. I've learned to respect the tensions and conflicts my students live with as they prepare to enter the teaching profession. Appreciating their student culture changes the way I work with them. I've never had a student capture my students' sense of being between worlds better than Allison. Her final words written in my class are a reflection on what she has learned with her peers, and a look forward to her future as a teacher:

> So I guess what this semester has done is make me whole again. It's made me feel stupid and it's made me feel superior. It's made me confident and it's caused me untold anxiety. I can't say that I'm sorry that it's almost over. I can say I feel ready to go on . . . and I'm going to miss it, too.

This is the way my students walk—three steps forward and two steps back. Sometimes they move gingerly, and other times they rush headlong into activities. One of the worlds they step into is my classroom. It is here that they will need to learn to respect their peers as colleagues. They will also spend time looking at how complex schooling has become, and how writing instruction has changed in the years since they were in elementary school. It's a lot to learn. The starting point is always writing workshops, where students begin to understand themselves as writers.

Three

Three Loves

Accident rules every corner of the universe except the chambers of the human heart.

— David Guterson, *Snow Falling on Cedars*

*T*eaching begins with love. My colleague Bill Cumming says we hesitate to mention love and teaching in the same breath. But this is where learning really begins. The word *love* conveys images of hearts and sounds mushy. I think of different kinds of love when I think of teaching, loves born of discipline and faith.

It has fallen out of favor to speak of work with teachers as teacher training. Teachers aren't dogs, after all. We prepare them, even test their mettle, but they aren't "trained." But I like the word *training* in the context of teacher preparation, because it makes me think of ballet dancers and figure skaters. Athletes and artists train daily. They push themselves, sweat, do the same routines over and over again, always aiming for an unattainable perfection of movement.

The kind of discipline and faith in ability that leads to such an intense daily regimen can't be sustained only by the thoughts of applause at distant performances. All those sore muscles, stress, failure again and again until a new skill is mastered—dancers and skaters must train out of love for what they are doing.

This weekend I watched the Olympic diving competition and I thought about teaching. Women walked to the edge of the board, poised on the very tips of their toes, and then jumped, twirled, flipped, and jackknifed into the water. Each dive was over in the blink of an eye. After leaving the water, every diver walked immediately over to her coach.

Those coaches didn't sit on the sidelines and relax with friends. They didn't say "good dive" or "bad dive" and then give the diver a slap on the back before she headed to the hot tub. After a while, the behavior of the coaches was more interesting to me than the diving.

It seemed that the divers really needed a response from their coaches. I realized the divers didn't have any kind of slow-motion camera in their mind's eye to tell them how the dive went. They depended upon the coaches to tell them what happened. And the coaches were very specific in their responses: "You cut that one a little low right from the start," or "Your hips were too far over the board in the jump." But it wasn't a distant, measured critique. You could tell the divers and their coaches had a strong bond, built out of day in, day out practice over a period of years.

The same coach would respond differently to the various divers he coached. I remember one response in particular. An American diver wasn't doing too well. She stood on the board, ready to attempt the most difficult dive in her program. It didn't have the highest difficulty rating of any dive she was attempting. But it was a reverse dive, and the commentator said reverse dives were always her failing.

She did a good dive. It wasn't a great dive, but there wasn't anything major wrong with it. The dive received decent scores. But you should have seen her coach jumping up and down! You would have thought she had just won the gold medal. He knew she was having a bad day and that this dive had been a major achievement for her.

That's the way it can be with teaching. A great achievement for one student is no great effort for another. Every student has a history. Sometimes when you are in the midst of a learning experience, it's hard to know where you are. It's hard to get perspective on your own work. Like the diver on the edge of the board, students are often balancing the risk involved in learning with many other concerns about form and context. They don't have the time, or often the ability, to analyze their growth and changes as learners. They may intuitively be doing the right things, but they don't yet have the ability to bring those intuitions to the conscious level.

As I watched the competition, I tried to imagine a different role for the coach. I imagined the diver coming out of the pool, and the coach holding up a little card with a number rating the dive. If the card said 5 or 10 or 7, I suppose the diver would learn something. She might learn that some of her dives were better than others. But without a personal, careful response, I wonder how she could become a better diver. The challenge to any teacher is to give the best response in each unique situation, to know when to criticize and when to celebrate growth. The commitment to the sport has to be fueled by love.

When I enter a methods class, my goal is to build that relationship of committed students and committed coach in the writing workshop. I know my relationship to each student will need to be focused, individualized, specific. At the same time, I will need to help them find their way into larger communities of students and teachers who share a commitment to learning born of love.

Real love sustained over time is alternately thrilling, draining, and demanding of constant attention. I have identified three loves that are critical in my teaching. These are a love of structure, a love of response, and a love of surprise. These loves are woven throughout my methods classes.

A Love of Structure

The most important thing I do as a teacher is think about structure. Good teachers are constantly questioning, playing with, and analyzing class structure. We are what we do. And the physical environment we work in plays a key role in determining the limits of our ability to build a structure that helps people learn.

Aesthetics matter. It's hard to learn in a place that's an eye-sore on the landscape, where ceilings leak and tiles are broken. Yet we expect students to learn in such places, whether they are six years old in their first school experience, or sixty years old returning to a graduate class after a forty-year break from college life. The physical plants of so many educational institutions speak to the hypocrisy of how highly our society says it values learners and learning.

When I first drove up to the University of Maine for my job interview, I surprised my host by saying, "I know which building houses the College of Education" and pointing to it. She asked in surprise, "Did you see the building in our catalogue?" I didn't have the heart to tell her it's easy on any campus to find the education college—it is invariably the ugliest building around. At Maine, the building stands out because it is brick with fading turquoise panels, a favorite motif briefly in the late 1950s and early 1960s, echoing the style of many elementary schools our students will work in. From a distance, the view of half-open windows and half-pulled shades gives the illusion that some of the windows are broken. This isn't the case, but it isn't a pretty picture. Almost all other buildings on campus are solid brick, with some ivy cover.

Our facade is typical of the education buildings on campuses I've visited. Once I visited a colleague's office on the campus of a small private college. I remarked upon how pretty the education department was, a low-slung older building with arches leading to small vestibules of offices. It was rare for educators to be given such a lovely environment to work in. She noted that the college was originally a private estate that had been converted to a college years ago. The education department had once been the stables of the estate, which accounted for the unusual architecture.

I worked for two years in another college of education that felt like a climate-controlled tomb. With high dark walls of cement, floors of marble, every footstep echoing down long hallways, and a temperature that always felt chilly, it was hard to feel the heat of passionate debate over new teaching theories.

So when I enter the classroom for the first class meeting in the fall, I've already fought a few battles because of my love of structure. We're meeting in one of only two classrooms in the building that have tables, not those awkward desk/chair combinations that don't allow for group work. We're meeting in the morning, because that's when students and I will be freshest. And we're meeting for three hours, twice a week, so we can take time to play with the structure and wander down unexpected avenues that emerge as we work together. But the room is still bare, it's not really mine or the students', and the real structure that matters will have to emerge from the routines that are established right from the start.

We always begin class on the first day with a workshop. I try to do as little talking as possible at the start. Annie Dillard (1989) writes that the most crucial decision for any writer is what to leave in and what to leave out. The most crucial decision for me as a teacher every day is when to talk and when to shut up. I know that it's much harder to listen than it is to talk, and I also know that the teacher and a few individuals tend to dominate in whole-class discussions. The structure of the class has to allow for lots of small-group time. Our whole-class discussion periods in writing and reading workshops are no longer than ten minutes most days, and this will be true also on the first day. The typical structure of the workshop includes:

- Opening with student reading or mini-lesson (3–5 minutes)
- Silent writing (10–15 minutes)
- Small-group discussions (30 minutes)
- Whole-class discussion (10–15 minutes)

Nancie Atwell writes of how she starts the first day of her workshop with writing, involving students in her own process. I've often started the first day of the semester with a similar routine. We begin with a brief lesson about writing,

35

some silent writing, and some small-group discussion of what's been written. It's important for me that we don't start with a syllabus, books required, or assignment due dates. I'm looking for "mindfulness" throughout the semester in students and myself—a concentration on the task or issue at hand that shows our full attention and careful thought. You can't have that mindfulness on the first day if six of your students are worried about the price of the textbooks, four are wondering how they will be graded, and seven are comparing the syllabus to the one from the class they just left. So I bury the syllabus for the first hour or two in my stack of class materials.

As soon as possible, we are writing quietly. Sometimes we have an activity as a way into the writing. One of my favorites is to have students draw a floor plan of a house they remember well, writing in the margins of the chart paper favorite sights, sounds, and memories. From the margins come writing possibilities, and eventually the silent writing. Sometimes students share stories that have been passed down in their families for years. From their family lore come connections to others in the class and a sense that they do have stories they have thought enough about to write about.

I need the silent writing as much as my students. Joan Countryman (1992), a well-known expert in math instruction, has her high school students write silently at the start of each class for a few minutes. She doesn't expect that the writing will be about issues with the current math assignment, or even about math at all. She finds the writing helps students "clear their heads" of all the stuff that's happened outside of class, so that they will be free to concentrate on what will be learned that day.

After all the fits and starts of signing registration forms and checking out stocks at the bookstore and saying hello to returning colleagues and hauling school supplies and getting a new parking sticker and all the other details of beginning a semester, I need those few moments early in the class to remind myself of why we're here. It's about writing, and learning to teach. Writing any narrative requires a concentration on the task at hand and immediately creates a mindfulness in all of us—a sense of place and the glimmers of possibilities for what we might be as a community by the end of the semester.

After students have written quietly for ten or fifteen minutes, I have them underline a phrase, sentence, or paragraph they like in their piece. Then it's time for the first writing response group. I want students to reach the point where they can respond incisively, thoughtfully, and tactfully to their peers' work. But many have never been in a writing response group. They are overwhelmed at the thought of reading their work to someone else. I read them these words by Ruth Nathan (1991, 19):

> If you are a teacher, holding a conference with a writer is not easy. The problem is twofold. Authors break easily, and teachers tend to criticize. Authors, especially authors who happen to be children, do not want advice right away. Authors want readers to tell them they've done a good job. Recently a fourth grader put it rather simply: "I want people to say, 'Oh, that's excellent.' "
>
> Authors understand that advice, while necessary, must be given at the right time and by a trusted individual. Because this is so, it is essential that you write if you are going to be a good writing teacher. It doesn't really matter that you write well; that's almost (but not totally) irrelevant. What does matter is that you attempt to write something well, and then that you read your draft to someone else. In other words, practice putting yourself on the line. It is knowing how a writer feels when a piece is shared, the chemical twang, the wildly beating heart, the mental involvement, the "I'm out there and feeling vulnerable" sensations that you must comprehend if you want to do a decent teaching job.

I give them a structure for response. The writer will read her work, and the responders will think about what they would have underlined as a favorite part. If time permits, they can also talk about what they want to learn more about from the writer. I emphasize specificity and that each writer must actually *read* his or her work, not summarize what has been written or pass it to a peer to be read silently.

I talk about how much harder it is to listen than it is to talk. I cite the physiology research that shows how body temperatures rise slightly and muscles quicken as people listen intently. As the groups work, I circulate, trying to say as little as possible.

After students have finished responding in groups, I usually have another five to ten minutes of silent writing, so that writers can work immediately from the advice given by classmates.

When silent writing has ended, we talk about the process. Students note what they liked and didn't like during the activity, how different parts of it made them feel. But lots of direct instruction in how to write is also going on. One woman talks about how it was hard for her to reenter her piece for the second period of silent writing. I tell her that writers often stop their writing of a draft in the middle of a sentence, so that they can go back readily into their train of thought at the time by having to finish the sentence. Another student talks about the warm memories another writer's piece evokes. We talk about how the mention of food in that piece makes it come alive—the Rice Krispies® treats evoke a time and place. I mention that odors are a powerful sensory device and a great tool for writers.

Another student talks about how she got stuck trying to remember if the barn in her narrative was red or gray. I note that journalists use the marker "tk" to leave a space where they're not sure of a word or information. It allows the writer to keep on with the story, instead of getting bogged down in a detail.

Another student talks about how hard it is for her to get anything on the page, and how she has always been a procrastinator. I give her the advice of the poet William Stafford (conveyed to me by way of Donald Murray) to lower her standards. What's in her head will always flow more beautifully than what lands on the page. All writers have to get something on the page, even if it is junk. Only then can you begin crafting and revising.

A student responds to this with her process—drawing a sketch of the house didn't lead to any writing, but it led to strong memories of the adventures on the lawn at her grandparents' house. She talks about how she was surprised at where the writing led her.

A man notes that in reading his draft to his classmates, he used the same word three times in the first paragraph. He didn't realize how awkward the early writing was in his piece. I talk briefly about a principle from physics—it always takes much more energy to get a system into motion than it does to keep it running. The leads are often awful in a first draft, but students of all ages are hesitant to revise them, because it was so hard to get those first words on the page. I make a mental note to do a mini-lesson at the start of the next class on leads.

On and on it goes. Many teachers who lecture at students mistakenly believe that a workshop format is unstructured. A closer look reveals that workshop formats are often the most highly structured learning environments in schools. By the end of the semester, I won't be giving any explicit guidelines for how these students should respond to each others' work in writing workshop. But there will be many different structures and strategies they test out, like the underlining and responding strategy of the first day's workshop, before they discover the strategies that work best for their group. Every group will have worked out its own means of responding, but the students will receive many structural possibilities throughout the semester.

The least complicated structure is a lecture presentation. It's much more difficult to allow lessons about writing to emerge from the needs of the group. By the end of a ten-minute whole-class discussion, I've given five micro-mini-lessons, including information on how to return to a draft, how to keep the narrative flowing when you're missing information, what senses are most evocative in writing, the paradox of lowering standards, the challenge of leads in a first draft.

It's exciting and frustrating at the same time. For every piece of information I know about writing that I can provide to students, there are dozens more that I haven't uncovered yet. Many of these will be provided by the students to each other—I always learn new things about writing through how these students talk about their drafts. It's a far different feeling than presenting a set of writing strategies with a quiet class dutifully taking notes. There is a sense that each class, even after the first hour of meeting, already has a life of its own.

I believe lots of writing about workshops still represents what is easy to document. We generate lots of articles and books about different formats for literacy workshops and different ways of keeping records. The hardest part of a workshop is that one-on-one, small-group, and whole-class teaching in the midst of the students. Many teachers read our literature about writing and reading workshops and mistakenly believe all you have to do is set aside the time for workshops, make sure students have timed individual, small-group, and whole-class writing and reading sharing sessions, and the workshop will go well. The false assumption is that the teacher's job is to keep good records and ask the right generic questions in conferences.

I think good teaching is like fishing. I don't like to fish, but my husband does. One of the reasons he will stand in a freezing stream from dawn to dusk is that he never knows what will happen next. He has to be ready, with all his skill from years in streams and lakes, hopeful that he has just the right lure and grade of fishing line to get the fish. But each fish will be a bit different. You can make generalizations about species, but when you face a wily fish you still need to summon all you know from past experience and books. Sometimes the fish leads, sometimes you lead. And there are many that get away.

The "teaching" in writing workshops in most textbooks is contained within the mini-lesson at the start or end of the workshop. I need more stories of the teaching in the midst, those very brief discussions with students that try to reach them when they are most ready to receive advice.

I honestly don't know which of the snippets of information I gave to students during that first whole-class discussion reached individuals. I don't know which sentences were pithy and to the point, and when I was blathering on with students completely lost. But it's the best representation I have of my struggle with the fish in that moment of class, and it is those moments that will define much of the structure in the class and my role in it in the coming weeks.

Those moments of teaching are also the piece of the structure that are easiest to love. My husband doesn't fish because we need food. He braves some amazingly awful conditions because no two days of fishing are ever alike. You never know what the fish are going to teach you about landing them, and under the water are untold possibilities.

Much of the writing about literacy workshops in our profession now feels a little flat to me because we've ignored those pieces of the structure that are the easiest to love—the moments when we actually have to instruct directly. I draw on everything I know in those moments from my experiences as writer and teacher, and it's not nearly enough. But it's why I keep coming back to the classroom year after year. My eyes glaze over when I read yet another way to chart student conferences or organize student portfolios. I want more hooks, lures, insights, and failures in the midst in our stories from writing workshops.

A Love of Response

I've never called myself a whole language teacher, and process teaching really doesn't explain what I do, either. Whole language classrooms and process workshops operate with many of the principles I believe in and practice, but the terms mean such different things to different teachers. I think of what I do as response-based teaching, or responsive teaching. I've seen these terms in the literature, but they aren't known enough to be in the lexicon of most educators. Response to students is at the heart of what I do. Like the students of the diving coach, my students need immediate, specific, and thoughtful response to their needs.

I find I need to respond to students in a variety of ways. Some students work with me best through conferences. Others find a written dialogue helps them overcome shyness. No assignment has ever met every student's needs. But with a range of dialogues available to each student, almost every one eventually establishes a conversation with me.

When I first began to teach undergraduates almost ten years ago, response to students consumed me. I wrote two pages of typed response to each student, each week. I spent hours crafting one response to a particularly thorny issue. There were many seventy-hour weeks in those first two years of college teaching. I now see I spent so much time in written response to students because I had so much to learn from them.

I still have lots to learn from students, and the individual dialogues at all levels are the key to the learning. But oh, those first semesters! Every presentation was new, and most of what I advocated was nowhere in evidence in the schools they visited. I was only a few years older than my students. I remember spending the entire summer before my first university job putting together presentations and materials for the undergraduate methods class. Those materials lasted all of two weeks.

I sometimes look back on those days with a touch of longing when I survey the boxes of examples of children's work in my office now, with files of overheads overflowing the file cabinets. But the longing doesn't last, because I remember how hard it was to work from a bare office, to scramble to find something to say.

My belief in response-based teaching started from working with professors who spent hours responding to my work. But it grew when I became a faculty member, because I was so needy myself. Those long letters were a challenge to students to tell me what I needed to know to help them. Many of the students were amazed and overwhelmed by my response, and they rose to the challenge by teaching me—about their culture, about their school experiences, about the kinds of classroom activities that helped them and those that didn't.

There's been a lot written about the incredible intensity of the first year of teaching. It's no different for university faculty who care about their students. But I knew I couldn't sustain that sort of intensity if I wanted a life outside my teaching. I needed a life outside of teaching, and my students needed me to have one, too.

I began to realize this in my first year of teaching. I remember one night I was up till 11 o'clock writing responses to students. I then spent three hours at the laminating machine, putting together a curriculum planning activity that involved grids and tiny strips of laminated resources that went into paper bags. I had devised the activity, and I thought it was nifty.

By the time I met with my class the next night, I was exhausted. I'd put in a twelve-hour day of teaching and meetings. I dragged myself to class with my stack of student responses, my little brown bags of laminated strips, and high hopes that this class would transform their view of curriculum planning.

The activity bombed. This was a terrific group of students, one that went happily down any path I led them. Within a few minutes of working with the grids and the paper bags, they were hopelessly lost. I was so tired it was hard for me to even remember what I wanted them to do with all those silly little tags. But that didn't stop me from feeling an anger rising in me. I'd worked so hard on this, stayed up half the night getting ready for the class. I looked down and saw the Band-Aid on my middle finger where I'd rubbed the skin on a knuckle raw from using the scissors to cut up those strips. Good grief, I'd even bled for this class! By the time the class was over, we all had a good laugh and a good conversation about what happens when students don't respond well to an activity the teacher has worked hard to create.

I realized over time that someone who stays up till all hours writing responses and slaving over a hot laminating machine isn't the best role model for students who want to know how they can be fine teachers and still have a balanced life.

I've spent much time as a teacher over the past few years wrestling with the issue of responsive teaching within a balanced life. In many ways, I'm a much better teacher than I was when I first worked with students. My students still receive individual and specific response each week, but I've learned to budget my time, to weigh the investment of time in certain activities against the return.

In all of my responses to students, I try to remember these words from Donald Murray (1987), the father of the conference approach to teaching. They are especially apt when I don't know how to respond.

> How should we respond to student writing? How should we respond to a look, a piece of blackberry pie, a kiss, a death in the family, a joke, to the sneaky warmth of the winter sun when it touches a hand?
>
> As a human being. As a human being who also writes. As a human being who writes and wants to help.
>
> To me a draft is a living thing. It is a piece of human communication—an embryo of understandable experience—that deserves its own life. It must be respected for its own possibilities. It must be nurtured, cultivated, cared for, delighted in.
>
> There can be no way—no single, correct, preconceived way—for one human being in the dynamic, ever-changing context of a human interaction to respond to another human being.

I try to respond to student writing with these words in mind, but I also often substitute the word *teacher* for writer. I respond to students as a human being—a human being who teaches and who wants to help my students teach.

I try to meet with every student for a quick conference in my office every two weeks, with the first conference the first week of class. I need to know what's going to get in the way of their learning over the semester—an unresolved struggle to find day care for a child, a too-heavy class load, financial problems that may cause a student to drop out. These quick initial conferences resolve so many small problems before they blow up. It's also hard to care about students before you know them. These conferences help me know my students better fast. I schedule them for ten or fifteen minutes during my office hours. I will be in my office at these times anyway, so the conferences fit into my quest for a balanced life and reasonable work hours. I only do these conferences every two weeks, because I couldn't sustain the intensity of the experience every week. I am exhausted after the days when I have had long hours of student conference after conference, but I have learned so much. Again, Donald Murray (1982, 41) says it best:

> It was dark when I arrived at my office this winter morning, and it is dark again as I wait for my last writing student to step out of the shadows in the corridor for my last conference. I am tired, but it is a good tired, for my students have generated energy as well as absorbed it. I've learned something of what it is to be a childhood diabetic, to raise oxen, to work across from your father at 115 degrees in a steel-drum factory, to be a welfare mother with three children, to build a bluebird trail, to cruise the disco scene, to be a teenage alcoholic, to teach invented spelling to first graders, to bring your father home to die of cancer. I have been instructed in other lives, heard the voices of my students they had not heard before, shared their satisfaction in solving the problems of writing with clarity and grace.

Many of my students thrive on a similar individualized approach to solving the problems of teaching. It's only one type of dialogue we will have, but it's a crucial one.

I've also used one form or another of journals in almost every class I teach. I was a student in the 1970s, when the use of journals first came into vogue. Almost every English or education class I took required a journal. I loathed this assignment. There were weeks when I cheated, lining up a series of different colored pens or pencils the night before the journal was due, then carefully writing out entry after entry, switching pens every so often and slanting my handwriting this way and that to give the illusion that I was dutifully sitting down once a day to record a big thought in my journal.

I don't think now that I was an evil and lazy student when I was cheating. I've come to realize that student responses make sense. Those journal assignments lacked meaning for me. When assignments lack meaning for students, they will give the assignment minimal effort. I would hand the pages in once every two weeks or once a month, and the assignment would come back with "good job!" or "interesting questions!" scrawled across the top. Even teachers who do respond in the margins of journals tend to move toward these kinds of generic responses very quickly. I was journaled to death by the time I graduated from college, and many of my students are in the same state of journal mortis by the time they reach me.

I vowed if I did use journals with my students, they would receive a prompt and specific response. I don't write in the margins of student work, or even on the page at all, unless the piece is in the final stages of the editing process. Writing a response on a separate sheet forces me to respond in a unique way to each student. It also shows respect that their words *are* their words—once I write on the page, I'm also a part of the text. I find students tend to imitate this way of responding when they begin to work with children—writing responses on separate slips of paper and asking permission before they write anything on the page.

My vow to do things differently with journals led to many of those seventy-hour weeks early in my teaching career. But they were a powerful tool for learning.

It's impossible for me to sustain the discipline of writing a response to every entry of every student each week and still respond to other work they do. It isn't a model that will work in many public school settings, either. I needed to demonstrate individual response in a way that could be imitated when students reached their student teaching and first-year positions.

I often start the semester with a daily journal requirement, and I write a one-page response to each student each week for the first four to six weeks of the semester. Then we move on to other kinds of writing and response. I make sure I write an individual response to each student in some way every week.

Lately I've enjoyed using quick-write dialogue journals in many classes. I take manila folders and staple lined paper inside. Students draw a line down the middle of the page and write to me on one side at some point before, during, or after class. I write back before the next class. They never take these journals home, and neither do I. It's a wonderful way to do a gut check of what is and isn't going well in the class, and they help me as a teacher researcher of my own students. Students use these journals to take care of minor questions and concerns in class, to respond to something I've said or written, or to expand on ideas or issues in their work.

Throughout the semester, these quick-write journals let me know immediately which students are struggling with the reading, who's grappling with a sudden personal emergency, what's said in a small group that angers or annoys. I write my responses in the odd free moments during the day, dragging a few journals to lunch or faculty meetings to write in while I wait. It usually doesn't take more than forty-five minutes to respond to thirty of these journals.

When I had students write daily journals outside of class and turn them in weekly, often it was two weeks from the day the journal was written to the day they received a response from me. And this was with my faithful commitment to get the journals back within a week. It was too long a gap of time for genuine dialogue to take place.

The other type of writing and response that has worked well is a one-page, single-spaced typed response that each student writes for each class in response to one of the readings. Students make four to five copies for small-group discussions. I have students read these papers silently in the small group and then give specific responses to ideas from each writer. I've adapted my guidelines for how the papers should be written from the work of Linda Rief (1992, 276–7):

Weekly Reading Responses

You are required to write a *one-page, single-spaced typed response* to one of the required reading assignments each week. *You need to make five copies*—one for each member of your response group and one for me. These responses will serve as a starting point for class discussions of the readings, and they will also help you think harder about what you're reading in the class. Some of the ways you might choose to respond include the following:

Quoting or pointing out: Quote a part of the book you feel is an example of good writing—a sentence, a paragraph, a long passage, a phrase. What did you like about this writing?

Asking questions: What confuses you? What don't you understand? Why do you think the author did something in a particular way?

Sharing experiences/memories: Does the writing remind you of anything? What comes to mind as you are reading this book? Write about these experiences or memories. What made you think of them?

Reacting: Write about your reactions to the book, giving examples and reasons for your reactions. Do you think the author was hoping you'd have this response?

Connecting: How does the article or book relate to other things we've already read? How do you predict you will use it in the future? What will it mean for your teaching?

This assignment should be considered a focused free-write. Think hard about the text but try to limit your actual writing time to less than an hour.

This assignment works on many levels. Discussions are richer in these groups because students have already thought about the materials. Over time, they begin to have a few good "voices in their minds," a continuing conversation with their classmates as they complete these papers class after class. I always write a response, too, and this keeps me involved in all the discussions. It also keeps the assigned readings fresh for me. I'm rereading each semester as a member of a different community.

The written responses allow every voice to be heard and different voices to emerge. Some students who are very shy, even in a small group, will write eloquently and passionately in these papers. Other folks with strident voices find they can't help but temper their views as they anticipate group reaction. I write a response to each of these brief papers on a Post-it note and return the assignment during the next class session.

None of these assignments is overwhelming to the students or me, and I get a sense of what mode works best for each student. Some prefer conferences, others like the instant debate of the journals, and many enjoy the collective response to the reading reactions. I tell students we are in the "practice school of writing," and I read them the words of Natalie Goldberg (1986, 11):

Writing as a Practice

This is the practice school of writing. Like running, the more you do it, the better you get at it. Some days you don't want to run and you resist every step of the three miles, but you do it anyway. You practice whether you want to or not. You don't wait around for inspiration and a deep desire to run. It'll never happen, especially if you are out of shape and have been avoiding it. But if you run regularly, you train your mind to cut through or ignore your resistance. You just do it. And in the middle of the run, you love it. When you come to the end, you never want to stop, and you stop, hungry for the next time.

That's how writing is, too. Once you're deep into it, you wonder what took you so long to finally settle down at the desk. Through practice you actually do get better. You learn to trust your deep self more and not give in to your voice that wants to avoid writing. It is odd that we never question the feasibility of a football team practicing long hours for one game; yet in writing we rarely give ourselves the space for practice.

When you write, don't say, "I'm going to write a poem." That attitude will freeze you right away. Sit down with the least expectation of yourself; say, "I am free to write the worst junk in the world." You have to give yourself the space to write a lot without a destination. I've had students who said they decided they were going to write the great American novel and haven't written a line since. If every time you sat down, you expected something great, writing would always be a great disappointment.

The rule that matters is that none of us can skip practice. We must write every day, and it's important, too, that we manage to write the minimal length requirements for that reading reaction. A runner can't quit a six-mile run after one mile—she needs discipline. I am also in the practice school of response. I know that I will get better at it as I am disciplined to do it.

I tell the students that some days their writing will be wonderful, and some days it will be just awful. But like the runner, they will see improvement and gradual changes over time.

I also need the regular and varied response to maintain a healthy relationship with my students. Donald Murray (1987) once told me he needed weekly conferences with his students, and I asked him to explain. He said,

> It's like those long-distance marriages. I've never understood 'em. I know some people can live apart from their spouse, fly in once a week or once a month, have a great exciting weekend, up all the time, and it works for them. That could never work for me. I have good days and bad days. I would worry that my bad day would fall on the one day of the month I saw my spouse. What would that do to the marriage?!

I understood him immediately. I have good days and bad days in response, too. Some conferences are wiped out because I'm just too tired from being up the night before with my baby or because I'm preoccupied with a class I have to teach in an hour. Other days my written responses to students are flat—I have little to say, and what I do eke out isn't worth saying.

I respect colleagues who can write responses to students once a month or twice a semester and with these detailed, articulate responses meet the needs of their students. But I couldn't depend on myself to be up or truly in tune with students when those assignments came in. By my having something to respond to every day, students are sure to catch at least a few incisive remarks on my good days.

I also need to write to students so that I can do writing like this—the professional writing that is part of my job. Writing to students is my way of limbering up for longer runs. For example, before I began on the draft of this book today, I wrote my reading reactions for next week's readings. That took about twenty minutes. I also wrote three Post-it responses to short papers from students—another ten minutes. Writing to students is a great warm-up for other writing tasks. Almost every idea in anything I've written about teaching can be traced back to a response I gave orally or in writing to a student.

After years of experimenting and tinkering, I love the many options my students and I have for responding to each other. But I also know that I will always be trying out new assignments for response as my students let me know what is and is not working for them.

A Love of Surprise

Teaching is full of surprises. Some surprises are delightful, and some make your head and neck ache. One of the most exciting and sometimes terrifying aspects of teaching is that you never know what is going to happen. I want my students to learn to look for what surprises them in classrooms and then ferret out the roots of the frustration or joy that the surprise brings.

Annie Dillard in *The Writing Life* (1989, 70) presents an incident where a student asks if she can someday be a writer:

A well-known writer got collared by a university student who asked, "Do you think I could be a writer?"

"Well," the writer said, "I don't know. . . . Do you like sentences?"

The writer could see the student's amazement. Sentences? Do I like sentences? I am twenty years old and do I like sentences? If he had liked sentences, of course, he could begin, like a joyful painter I knew. I asked him how he came to be a painter. He said, "I liked the smell of paint."

I want my students to learn to like the smell of the paint, the dailyness of teaching—the minor incidents and encounters that startle teachers every day, that capture the spirit of how learning and communities are built over time. I want them to like the ordinary—those good and bad surprises that come moment by moment in any classroom. That love of surprise is what will help them continue to learn their craft, incident by incident, long after they leave me.

Learning to teach was a process of learning to see for me. I couldn't smell the incidents that mattered when I began to teach and observe teachers. So much was happening in the classrooms I visited, but I had no focus for seeing or explaining what was going on.

I had almost no teaching experience when I entered Pat McLure's first-grade classroom as an observer a dozen years ago. I walked in, saw lots of children reading and writing together, a happy hum of learning. Nice. The earth didn't move. I figured I'd see what I needed to see in a few days or weeks to understand that classroom and the way Pat teaches.

I left three years later, frustrated because I knew there was so much more for me to learn. Over the first days, weeks, and months in that room, I think I really learned to see classrooms for the first time by watching how Pat saw her students.

I remember Eric, a student I couldn't help but notice in my first days in that classroom. In September, Eric would try to spend almost every morning writing period wandering around the room. Any prod from Pat for a little more time on task was met with his standard "you must hate me" glare. He would then sit down at a desk, head in hands, a heavy sigh emerging from his tiny chest. After a few moments, a few illegible words would be scrawled across the page. By the time anyone asked Eric to read what he had written, he would respond, "I can't remember and I don't care." I watched Pat work with him day after day, sometimes ignoring his tears at her firm commands, sometimes hugging him when he was able to read what he had written.

I also noticed the way Pat talked about Eric. Some days she

was discouraged and shared her discouragement. And yet, many more of her observations were positive. There were no real generalizations about Eric in those first weeks. Every day brought an event with Eric that we would mull over together. Like the writer who painstakingly builds his story sentence by sentence, a portrait of who Eric was as a learner began to emerge, incident by incident. By looking closely, there was as much delight as frustration in coming to know him.

I began to see what a keen eye for detail Eric himself had through Pat's own keen eye for detail. One day, Eric noticed how much slimmer his writing folder was than another student's (because he was producing little work). "Why, this folder looks like a dog that died and got sucked right flat!" he declared. When a dead but lovely butterfly was brought in for the science table, Eric told me, "She died because she just flew and flew and she didn't take the time to eat her suppers." I realized it's easy for me also to fly and fly distractedly around a student like Eric, racking my brain for solutions to his "problems." I learned I had to take time, as his teacher did, to be nourished by his good qualities—his eagerness to share what he was seeing, his ability to turn a phrase or create a metaphor in an instant. Slowly but surely, Eric talked his way into steady improvement in his writing. More important for me, he helped me learn to see with a teacher's eyes.

In the late 1950s, an advanced form of cataract surgery helped many people see for the first time. Jacob Steinberg (Dillard 1989) was one of the researchers who did case studies of what vision was like for these newly sighted people. He and others were flabbergasted at what these people saw. One woman described the view as blobs of color, "without form or function." Another could not discern the difference in size between a walnut and an armchair.

The researchers were surprised at the depth and complexity of their findings. Until they worked with these newly sighted people, they had no concept of how much of sight is learned through our culture. The youngest babies are being taught implicitly and explicitly about what is important to perceive in the environment, and what must be ignored. Learning to see was a painstaking collaborative task for the patients and doctors. Not all patients enjoyed the new perspective they had on the world.

For all the time they've spent in classrooms, future teachers are like those newly sighted people in Steinberg's study. In many respects, they don't yet know how to see as teachers need to see. And why should they? Many classrooms that they've experienced as students are dreary, prefabricated places. There is a flatness, a uniformity in presentation of information. The view they've seen of teachers through their students' eyes is of someone looking out at a sea of faces, often with little interest in discerning differences.

Unfortunately, many methods classes reinforce this view of instruction by placing so much emphasis on rigidly detailed lesson planning. Requiring students to construct a fourteen-page plan of objectives and strategies for what they will teach for an hour to an imaginary group of students tells prospective teachers that there isn't anything they need to see first to be able to teach. This kind of lesson planning also teaches them that any kind of surprise is the worst calamity because it forces teachers to deviate from the plan.

The thing I hate most about these lesson plans, beyond the ways they blind students to the individual needs of students and teachers, is that they make future teachers believe that planning for instruction is a dreaded and dreadful task. Lesson plans foster a justified cynicism in new teachers. They learn planning is a game you play, to please your professor who will probably never see the plan in action and with the goal of one day pleasing an administrator who will rarely take the time to understand how you make daily classroom decisions.

Planning is my favorite part of teaching. I sort through papers, texts, and old presentations, and play with options for many days over the summer or breaks, when I consider all the possibilities for what students and I might do during the semester, weighing that against what I feel we must do. I talk about the options with colleagues and former students; I argue with myself about what might work. Nothing could be more energizing or exciting. Playing with the structure of class is part of planning. Figuring out how I'll respond to students is part of planning. But I also accept that most of the planning must take place in the midst, as I work with students, and see what it is they need.

Classroom structure, understanding teaching, linking plans to student needs—it all comes back to knowing what you're looking for and how to make sense of it. In place of creating detailed lesson plans, much time is spent in the class in conscious and deliberate effort to help students learn to see classrooms in new ways.

One of the best tools I have for developing sight are videotape segments of students and teachers in action. Most of my students have spent lots of time in front of a television set, perhaps even more time for some than they've spent in classrooms. In our television culture, we expect to sit back and be entertained when we watch television. The writing workshops in our class require structure to help students learn together. The same is true of viewing videotape segments of writing workshops in schools. Students need to be given structure, especially early in the semester, to learn how to look actively and learn from a classroom segment.

When I first showed videotape segments to students, I didn't give much of a structure for viewing them. My students' reaction to these segments was often much the same as my reaction when I first entered Pat McLure's room. Nice, but the earth doesn't move. Focusing on Eric sharpened my vision of everything happening in that room, and students need help in finding a focus. They need to look at those "ordinary" classroom sights again and find the surprises that will instruct them.

So now when I show a videotape of a second-grade student giving a tour of her classroom, I ask students to keep a running list of all the responsibilities students have in this classroom. I tell them to list mundane details like sorting books.

But I also ask them to look deeper at the rules and responsibilities, to notice things like the way students ask each other for permission before touching each others' work. Just two examples open up many windows for views into this particular classroom.

When a first grader is talking as he works on a piece of writing, I have students write down every sound or letter they notice him practicing. I can tell students that a writing workshop is an applied phonics program. But this concept doesn't come alive until they are surprised at the number of sounds a child plays and struggles with in a three-minute stretch, until they compare their lists and what they saw with what their classmates saw.

I help them focus on something in the tape, but I'm often surprised at what they learn. I think that's an important point, too—it's amazing how differently we view the same issues, and how we are able to learn different things even when using similar lenses.

It's important for me throughout the semester that the videotape segments we use be short. There is an intensity in looking closely, in trying to figure out what's important to see and what must be ignored for the moment. Once you do start looking closely, you are bombarded with possibilities on any videotape and in any classroom.

Beyond videotape and overhead examples of student work, the other part of learning to see and be surprised is learning to be a researcher. I have my students do more and more data collection in schools and in the local community. They interview whole groups of teachers, adults, and children, bring these interview results to class, and sift through the data. I believe teachers need to be researchers of their students and their own teaching process. So in our class we search and search again for the patterns within the learning processes of adults and children.

For example, in the first week of class each student interviews three adults with the Burke Writing Interview. Students bring in these interview responses. All responses for each question are compiled on large sheets of chart paper, and then students work in small groups to sift through the information and play with the data. They then organize the information into some sort of chart or graph. This is an activity we will use throughout the semester to help us all see the larger frame of whole-class and whole-culture views in different contexts.

My goal is to someday have a multimedia lab with CD-ROMs that contain many of my videotape examples of classrooms, masses of unanalyzed interview data from classrooms, reams of student writing, and audiotapes of literature and writing response groups. I know my students could sharpen their sight if they had more opportunities individually and in small groups to wander through these materials together, to find the patterns across schools, grades, and learners we just don't have time to explore together. I think the day that my dream becomes a reality is fast approaching. But until then we still find lots of pleasure in being surprised together as we see literacy emerge in ourselves and the many students on tape and overheads who become a part of our classroom life.

Falling in Love(s)

My hope is that my students will leave with some of the same loves I have for structure, response, and surprise. But I also know they will leave with many other loves born of the unique passions and experiences they bring to the craft of teaching.

English professor Peter Biedler (1986) may have said it best: "We've got to get our students to the point where they stop asking, 'Will this be on the test?' and start asking, 'Will this be like falling in love?'" As my students start learning from each other, start dialogues with me, start engaging with the texts, they begin to fall in love with all kinds of things—themselves as literate beings, as newly sighted kid watchers, as humane members of a classroom community. For many, it's the first time they've framed the value of a course in terms other than a grade.

When you love something, you invest a lot of energy in it. Passion drives people, and there is no time of more energy and intensity than in those first weeks or months when you are falling in love. When I evaluate what I do, the thing I most value is helping students fall in love with teaching writing. And watching them fall in love makes me fall in love all over again, every semester, with the joys and challenges of this profession.

Four

Two Students

*Quality . . . you know what it is, yet you don't know what it is
. . . But some things are better than others, that is, they have
more quality . . . but what's the "betterness"?*
— Robert Pirsig, *Zen and the Art of Motorcycle Maintenance*

In that old hippie classic *Zen and the Art of Motorcycle
Maintenance*, the character Phaedrus agonizes over the quality
of his instruction of freshman composition students. The word
"quality" haunts Phaedrus as he attempts to define it with his
students, and demonstrate it through their writing. In the
process, he argues with himself over defining it.

As someone who works with future teachers, I wonder
about the quality of my own work. All students complete the
same assignments, within a predictable workshop structure.
But students start out at different points on their *methodos*.
Though some of the checkpoints—their values and concerns—may be the same, the journey will not be exactly the
same for any one student.

Lucy Calkins has written that all writers have a few seminal
themes that they will return to again and again throughout
their work. I have found this is also true with my students.
Any student has a number of themes that show up time and
time again in their work. Many of these themes or concerns
develop before the students enter my class, and it's my job to
help students work their way through them.

Two of the most important goals in my writing methods
courses are to help students understand literacy through their

own reading and writing processes, and to place this under-standing within the context of their future as teachers. The writing my students do is linked to their lives. The challenge the students face is to see their lives as texts and their texts as lives. Because they come from different backgrounds, with different experiences and concerns, the journeys they take through that writing will vary greatly. The links between texts, lives, and quality of learning in the course are messy.

The best way to show differences in the journeys taken by students may be through case studies of the writing of two very different learners, Beth and Sharon. These case studies don't represent the routes all students take, but they do show how unique the learning in a methods course can be for different students.

Beth: Shaking Hands with Lenny

The story of Beth's quest for quality in her writing began out-side of my class. She attempted to enroll in a fiction writing course taught by Lenny Schwartz during the first week of the semester. Beth was surprised when she wasn't chosen for the course. "You don't know how much this affected me," she told me in an early conference. "I mean, I thought I was a good writer." She chose to write about the experience in her first journal entry for my class:

> Today I discovered that I was rejected from a fiction writing class. Forty people submitted writing samples, and the class had a ten-person limit. I also noticed that there were no girls' names on the list. I understand that the prof would prefer a small class, but I wonder why they can't add another section. How do you learn something when they won't let you in the class? I suppose if I were one of the ten, though, I might see things differently. I wonder how fair I will be as a teacher.... I think I'm mad at Lenny Schwartz—master of fiction writing.

For the rest of the course, poor Lenny Schwartz would ap-pear and reappear in Beth's journal, reading logs, and papers.

I want to emphasize that Beth wrote over one hundred pages of drafts during the course, and Schwartz was mentioned on no more than ten of those pages. If he had been a true obsession, I would have referred Beth to the counseling center. But rather than being an obsession, her experience with Schwartz showed up in her work as a kind of romantic leitmotif, helping her to focus her thoughts on who she is as a writer and who she might be as a teacher.

In the second paper she wrote for me and shared with her small group recounting her history as a writer, she described the experience of rejection more vividly:

> My name was not one of the ten listed on Lenny Schwartz's door. I read the list again, each name out loud this time, and did not hear my voice utter anything resembling "Beth O'Grady." The instructor of English 305, Introduction to Fiction Writing, had made a grave error. Didn't he recognize the literary genius underlying the story I had submitted? I had slaved for hours, delicately intertwining plots, and discretely setting moods. My characters were magnificent: Charles, the guy who delivered pizza on his motorcycle, and Angelica. Precious Angelica, the frustrated virgin trapped in a boat house, reevaluating her career choice as a Spanish teacher.

Beth defined Lenny's influence on her writing through the title she gave the piece: "Writer's Block /rit-erz 'blak/ vb 1: Lenny Schwartz." What miffed her most was the realization that Lenny Schwartz hadn't seen her work as satire; he had merely seen it as overwrought fiction. Much of Beth's sense of self was linked to her self-deprecating and caustic sense of humor. She felt Schwartz had been unfair to her, and so she was not exactly humane in her reactions to him. It was a simple, evil pleasure for her to learn that Schwartz's lone publication during the previous year had been a short story with the rather pathetic title, "Me at Thirteen: Fat, Sallow, and Callow." The combination of daily writing experiences and a rich fantasy life led Beth at times to turn her pen on Schwartz. Hell hath no fury like that of a woman writer scorned, as this excerpt from another paper reveals:

My fingers let go, and the envelope fell through the metal slot. Mail had piled up over the holiday weekend, so my carefully typed pages had a cushion to rest on. I had always wanted a pen pal, and even though mine never wrote back, it was still a satisfying relationship. I thought of him relaxing on his cot, or perhaps he was perched at the edge of a chair reading, relishing every sentence I had written, my words bringing vibrant color to the drab gray walls that surrounded him. Lenny would surely love this story! I hoped it would help him to pass the time in his cell.

Even though she joked about her recurring visions of Schwartz, being rejected from the fiction writing class forced her to reevaluate her sense of self and writing ability. For Beth, the two were closely linked.

Of course, Beth wasn't the only person in the class who was reevaluating her sense of self through her writing. One of the members of her first small writing group was Joe. Joe was in his mid-thirties, returning to school at night for certification and eking out a living by substitute-teaching during the day. In the first piece of writing he shared with his small group, he explored some of the choices he had made that had brought him to this point. When Joe was in college in the late 1960s, he planned to become a lawyer. Instead, he became immersed in the antiwar effort and transferred his allegiance from the ROTC to the SDS. His narrative is a poignant tale of sacrifices for causes and the strains this caused in his family. He closes with this challenge to the self-involved twenty-year-olds in his class:

> Even though fifteen years have passed, I continue to have strong feelings about the Vietnam War years. My father and I do speak now, but there is always going to be that large gap from the war years. I am no longer a radical, but I am still a freethinker with a mind of my own. . . . Those years were considered by many to be a time of romantic overtones when in fact those were chaotic and troubled times. . . . I like to look back and say that my generation was instrumental in stopping a war. What has yours done lately?

Beth took Joe's words to heart. In her third paper, there is no mention of Schwartz. Her paper is titled "An Attempt to

Reply," in which she sorts through her recollections of the Vietnam War period. The start of the piece is vivid and straightforward:

> So you see your generation as one that helped end a war, and you want to know what mine has done lately? I can't speak for my whole generation, of course, but I can tell you how I see things.
>
> Let me start from the perspective of a six-year-old girl, selling lemonade at the end of my driveway. It never failed, after selling one cup, I would spill the rest of the pitcher. I had one customer. Perhaps I would have had more if I could have kept the lemonade on the card table a little bit longer. He was always very nice to me, but we never had much of a conversation. He was a teenager, and I was six, so there wasn't much common ground for us to chat about. But he intrigued me, so I set out every nice day to provide him with a refreshing drink.
>
> My grandmother called him a hippie and blamed his long hair on the Beatles. "If it wasn't for the Beatles," she would say, "Then teenagers would still respect their parents!" It was all so fascinating, and I couldn't wait to grow up.

Beth goes on to explain how young and unaware she was during the Vietnam War. But as she approaches the present day, the narrative unravels. She tries to justify her peers' lack of involvement in politics, even as she states that they are activists in their own way:

> So here I am in my senior year of college. I've read a lot of books, and formed some questionable opinions. I'll soon be contributing to society by teaching children to read and write, but there's more to it than that. I'm from a generation that has finally begun to learn from past mistakes. . . . After decades [of Soviets and Americans] building up arms to intimidate each other, it has finally been realized that the answer is to give each other the benefit of the doubt. Students are being exchanged, and missiles are being destroyed. I see my generation as one that helped to end a war before it began. . . .
>
> I have never partaken in a protest. Extremists might consider that apathy, but I think there are better ways of handling many of the controversial situations facing us today. It seems to be in

vogue to throw yourself across the doorway of clinics performing abortions, and to leave thousands of children sitting in classrooms without teachers. I suppose I'll learn more about strikes and unions next year, but can't the bargaining be done over the summer? That may be a young and naive statement, but I make no excuses for that. Learning like all else, happens in its own time.

Beth's paper rambles on in this manner for over two pages. She jumps from topic to topic. Some of the insights connect, and some of them disagree with each other. She realizes this as she closes with these words:

> I don't think that I have sufficiently answered your question. The fact is, I have thought about this for more hours than you can imagine, and this series of disjointed thoughts is all I can come up with. . . . I think my peers and I are in a very egocentric period of our lives, all of us just trying to "get through." That's not to say we don't stop to take a look around, but we're still looking from the inside out. Can I get back to you on this in a few years?

Beth was convinced this was the worst piece of writing she had ever completed. She was surprised at the warm reception it received in class. Other students loved it, believing she had captured both the gap between generations and the sense of being between worlds that many of her peers felt.

With this narrative, Beth came full circle in understanding good quality in her writing. At the start of the term, she felt she was a good writer but an external judge had rejected her work. And in attempting to reply to Joe, she writes a piece she judges inferior. The rest of the class responds that it is of high quality indeed. Beth finds it messy and incomplete, but her peers remind her that their lives are, after all, also messy and incomplete.

In her final paper for my class, Beth has to evaluate what she has learned over the course through re-reading her work. She realizes how quick she is to judge others and how rampant her cynicism was early in the term. Her sense of humor, however, remains in full flower:

Looking back over various things I've written in the last three and a half months, there seems to be some evidence of hypocrisy. It's more prevalent in the pages from September and October, as I became progressively more aware of the cynicism that was obvious to others. I never paid much attention to it before, but I really don't want to sound condemning and closed-minded. I am pretty open to new ideas, I just judge them a little too quickly on occasion. Take basal readers for instance . . . I hate them. Have I ever used them for any length of time in a classroom? No, unless one week is considered a justifiable trial period. I do have reasons that back up my opinion, but I'm sure there are good reasons for using them that I have failed to seek out. Now let's talk about *teachers* that revolve their classrooms around basal readers.

I think they're _____ (lazy/cat).

I guess I still haven't conquered the sarcasm.

Perhaps more important, Beth sees her own evolution as a writer and thinker in terms of how she will teach other writers:

> In learning how to approach educating others to write, which is actually just giving them the opportunity to freely do so, I am learning to bring my own writing through an evolutionary process. The progression of writing is an intricate mixture of applying background knowledge to imagination. . . . Every individual has a unique voice that is not so much learned as it is matured through experiences and revision. . . .
>
> Becoming a "good" writer has been a goal of mine for a while now. It always seemed like a glamorous ideal, though. I wasn't really even sure what "good" writing was, I only knew what I liked and didn't like. I think I have become a better critic of myself, which has allowed me to take myself and my endeavors more seriously.

The free writing, choice, and wandering around topics in her writing for my class were necessary for Beth to understand, respect, and develop her own internal standards for good quality. The distance she travels as a writer can't be measured week by week, but only through the clear lens of three months' time.

Beth travels a long road in the course to come back a short distance—to Lenny Schwartz. In her final piece written for the class, an essay about what she has learned, she closes with an image of him:

> Cigarettes disgust me, but for some reason I have this image of myself ten years from now, smoking in a train station someplace, watching frantic people glance at their watches as they maneuver through crowds. In an effort to avoid a collision with a child's stroller, Lenny Schwartz bumps into me. I, a complete stranger to him in person, shake his hand and leave him standing there puzzled.

Beth imagines herself ten years from now traveling beyond Schwartz's rejection. But her personal *methodos*, the journey through writing she takes in our class, has allowed her already to deal with the rejection and move into larger issues of her place in the world as a socially responsible teacher of writers.

Sharon: The Now and the Not Yet

Sharon's journey begins from a different point. A student in her late thirties, Sharon was returning to school for certification. A theme that ran through Sharon's journey was the tension between her ideal vision of what she wanted to be as a teacher and the reality of her personal and professional limitations. Unlike some of the younger students in the class, Sharon had a clear sense of her work habits and abilities, and a longer history to draw on. She wrote early about her belief in innate ability, particularly when it comes to writing and teaching:

> After reading all these articles on writing, I'm still wondering if it's possible to teach someone to be a good writer. I do believe that it is possible to help people become more effective writers, but I believe that true talent is innate. It seems as though those who are truly gifted have unusual powers of observation, or expression or insights that others (like me) will never have.

Sharon also believed that the only hope for someone who lacked necessary abilities or knowledge was to receive them from someone else. I quickly learned in her first set of journal entries that I was to be one of these "important" others she would depend upon to fill her with knowledge, as she wrote in a subsequent entry:

> I'm scared! The reading and language arts courses I'm taking are the last reading and language arts courses I'll take before I student-teach. I need to learn everything a prospective teacher must know about these subjects from these two courses. Will these courses teach me all I need to know? Will I be prepared when I'm through? Will I retain everything I learn . . . until next spring when I student-teach? I hope you're a good teacher since twenty-six of us are depending on you to equip us for this challenge. I once heard it said that "teachers who prepare teachers for teaching should be the best there are." I wish that were true. Unfortunately I know that this is not always the case. Sometimes I finish a course and think, "I've learned so much from that person." Other times I think, "What exactly did I learn from that person that I couldn't have learned by myself?" You are so important to us. I truly hope you can rise to the occasion.

I love it when my students are blunt and honest in their early entries, because it allows me to adopt the same tone with them. In my response to Sharon's entry, I let her know I did not believe that what she learned or how she taught language arts was my sole responsibility:

> Oh, pull-lease. Give me a break here. There is no way you can possibly learn everything you need to know about language arts in one course. My goal is to expose you to all the resources you need to get you started. Most important, I want you to become excited about teaching language arts, so that you'll want to learn more as you teach. We are forever teachers in training. You never know enough to construct a perfect curriculum, or deal with the unique challenges students present. Me, rise to the occasion of teaching you? You rise first, and I promise to follow your challenges.

These entries were the start of a continuing debate, both in Sharon's head and across the page to me, about how much control she had over her future as a teacher. Could she maintain a positive attitude? Could she continue to be a learner in the schools? Sharon knew herself too well to believe that she would manage to maintain all her ideals, and she struggled to identify her own shifts in mood in envisioning her future:

> Today is an "I can't wait to be a teacher" day. When I wake up, I just never know if it's an "I'm scared" day or an "I can't wait to be a teacher" day. Some elementary school teachers have little calendars and every school day students chart the weather. I need a calendar on which to chart my feelings toward teaching.

🙂   this is my excited face

😟   this is my worried face

🙃   my wondering face

😐   my determined face

Sharon gave herself little tests throughout the term to see if she could meet her own goals and standards. She explored the tension she felt between the ideal and the real through these tests. One of the options in my class is to share a piece of writing with the whole class. Sharon challenged herself to share her writing one week, and she wrote a short pep talk in her journal to herself, trying to allay her fears in the situation:

> Well, I've decided to take the plunge! By the time you get to read this, it will be over. All the doubts, the uncertainty, the fears and apprehension will be gone. I'm going to put an end to these nagging thoughts and inferiority and take charge. As you read this, you will know that I have gone and done it. I will have shared my Brownie story with the class. My story is certainly innocuous. What do I have to fear? Certainly the students will not feel compelled to unite against me, to shun me, to force me into hiding or worse to kill me. My story is just about a car. It's definitely not the worst thing ever written—I've done worse. Just pick up the paper and read. Pretend you're sitting at the kitchen table reading to the coffee pot, the tea kettle, and the stove. I'll do it! I'll read to the class next Wednesday. I hope!

I read these words after the date Sharon had set for reading her work to the whole class had passed. I knew she hadn't chosen to share her writing that night. Later in her journal, she writes about her failure to meet that goal:

> Well, I'm going to write a poem about my ability to read to inanimate objects but my inability to read to people. Although I don't consider it a great piece, it's fun.
>
> *Sitting in my kitchen*
> *Reading to the pot*
> *Reading to the tea kettle*
> *And to the table top.*
>
> *Reading everything I write*
> *Listening quiet as can be*
> *Listening quite intently*
> *And never critically.*
>
> *Sitting in the classroom*
> *Paralyzed with fear*
> *Glancing all around me . . .*
>
> *I'm stumped for an ending. Maybe*
> *. . . Get me out of here*
> *. . . I wish people couldn't hear*
> *. . . Help*
>
> My group members decided on "Wishing people couldn't hear."

What's always interesting about reading Sharon's work is the tension in it. Sharon did share this poem with the whole class. And she relies on her small-group critique to help her with the ending, even as she believes she is hesitant to receive support. Like Beth, Sharon connects her own experiences to how she will work with young writers someday:

> I've been thinking about the poem I wrote yesterday and I'm struggling for an ending. As I sat looking at the poor poem without an ending, I thought of the line "I want to disappear." That seems to target my feelings about reading to the group. It's so easy to sit at the kitchen table and read out loud to all the objects sitting around. When it comes to people sitting around, that's an entirely different matter. I hope I can remember this when I become a teacher. Children should want to share not be forced

into it. I need to be sensitive and considerate of students' apprehensiveness just as I want to be treated. When the time is right and students feel confident about themselves and their work, they'll volunteer.

A difference between Sharon and other students is her experience in public schools. One of the greatest tensions present in Sharon's writing was the tension between her ideal vision of herself as a teacher and the many traps she could fall into, and had, in her past experiences in schools:

Riding to school today, I began to think about how much school means to me. I love school and I love everything about it. I love the mental and sometimes physical challenges, the friendships, the deadlines, and the sense of accomplishment. In a way, though, I'm fearful of becoming a teacher. Having worked in a public school for two years I know what it's like behind the scenes. Every day at lunch I sat in the teachers' lounge listening to teachers gripe about their students, about the principal, and about the teachers as well as about the administration. Don't get me wrong. I griped, too. You didn't fit in if you didn't. My second year at that school I stopped eating in the teachers' lounge and started eating at my desk. It was peaceful and quiet there. As I was going to school in the evening, I could study at my desk or just look out the window. I quit that job in August to return here full time. I really want to be a good teacher and I want my students to love school as I do, but I wonder if I'll love school under the conditions I mentioned above. Also I sometimes wonder about the quality of teachers themselves. In my math for elementary teachers [course], some of the students talk continuously while the instructor teaches. These are prospective teachers! At school here I can pick and choose my friends, and they are usually conscientious good students who will most likely become conscientious dedicated teachers. But I might be placed in a school with a group of teachers who are gripers and gossips. I realize that there are many conscientious teachers around. Sit in a teachers' lounge for 180+ days, though, and you begin to wonder where they are. It's bad to grow older because all the heroes of my youth have fallen from grace. Doctors, lawyers, priests, presidents, politicians, and teachers. Only a few select individuals remain, and I wait for their fall.

Reading Sharon's journal, I began to believe that the fall she waited for and feared the most was *her own*. She had big plans for her future as a writer and teacher, plans that developed throughout the term. She decided she would work with a friend to continue her writing throughout the summer:

> Recently a good friend came to visit. We began to talk about writing. She said that she had seen Kurt Vonnegut on TV. He said that there were two types of writers: "gushers" and "prodders." The gushers could sit down and the words just tumbled out. The prodders, however, inched along slowly. I believe that writers can be a combination of both depending on the assignment and the day. . . . We talked a lot about writing that day and decided to form a writers support group this summer. She is a PhD accounting professor and neither of us have time now, but we are very excited about this for the summer.

One day Sharon believes she can accomplish anything:

> I'm so excited inside that I feel like bursting because I know that I will be a good teacher. . . . When I first began my teacher certification program, I was uncertain about myself and my abilities. But now I'm so different. I feel so confident and excited that I can hardly wait till the day when I step into my own classroom. Every day I discover more about the kind of teacher I want to be and the kind of classroom I want to have. . . . I can't wait to share my enthusiasm about school and learning with my class.

But the very next day Sharon realizes the plans for the writing support group will probably turn out the same as her plans to share her "Brownie" story with the whole class. She knows herself too well:

> I will truly miss writing. I'm a lazy person who's not very self-disciplined. School is good for me because it has deadlines which keep me moving steadily ahead. Without deadlines I stagnate. Some people like to learn and read about things on their own. I have a friend who has often said that if she wants to learn about something she'll do it on her own. Not me. I lie around and watch TV. I'm like many special ed kids who need to stay in school all year because they regress when they have time off. I

need someone to stand behind me and shove me forward. That's why I'll miss writing, because I'm not sure I'll really do any more till someone "forces" me to. Even though my friend and I plan to have our writers support group this summer, she's exactly like me—lazy.

The tension between the ideal and the real for Sharon peaks in a journal entry in which she compares herself to a literary character:

> Of all the literary characters, the one I relate to mostly is Charley in *Flowers for Algernon* [Keyes 1966]. He was just a retarded store sweeper on whom an experimental drug was used. He became increasingly more intelligent and then the effects began to dissipate as he began to revert to his former self. For me the horror of this story is that Charley became bright enough to understand what was happening to him but powerless to control it. In that respect I feel much like Charley. I am smart enough to see what I want for myself. I want to be very bright and an accomplished writer. Yet I realize that I will never be what I want. Inside my head there seem to be two people always at odds, i.e., the person I am and the person I want to be. The "person that is" is in a constant state of turmoil and frenzy trying to prove to the "person I want to be" that the "person that is" is not dumb and unworthy.

I spent a lot of time thinking about Sharon's journals. She floats back and forth between aspiring to greatness as a writer and teacher, and accepting her limitations. Part of me says I should exhort her, trying to make her believe anything is possible. But the larger part of me knows she is writing truth. Perhaps this is because she is approaching middle age and she can admit the dreams of youth seldom take flight. This is what Thoreau was thinking about when he wrote, "The youth gets together his materials to build a bridge to the moon or perchance a palace or temple on earth, and at length the middle-aged man concludes to build a woodshed with them."

Is it good or bad to realize you will not achieve greatness? I already feel the grand dreams of *my* youth slipping away. They are being replaced with simple pleasures and challenges like driving home on a clear night after class and thinking about how Sharon connects her life to the character Charley. It's a short drive home, to a nondescript apartment, from a now empty classroom with bare walls. In the scheme of the universe, Sharon and I have a small-change existence. Even the best teachers seldom have their best moments in the classroom recognized or applauded.

It's hard to respond to Sharon, to let her know I understand how she feels. I need to let her know that it's all right to redefine greatness, to know that it's enough to appreciate your own best moments in the classroom. I settle upon a garden metaphor in my reply to her:

> Your analogy of yourself to Charley was so sad. I don't think anyone, even the most successful writer, ever measures up to the power of the words they hear in their head. In this way we are all Charleys. . . .
>
> You write about living an ordinary life and wanting to make a difference. I think the plot we each have to tend is very small. As long as you can make that garden of your classroom a delightful place, then you have made a spark. I don't aspire to much more than that, because when the garden grows well, it's enough to fill my whole world.

And Sharon does enjoy simple pleasures and possibilities. By her final journal entry, she seems to have reconciled herself to the ongoing tension between what she is and what she hopes she will be as a teacher. She seems to accept that there are many possibilities for fulfillment, personally and professionally, and that only she will fully understand those possibilities and the choices she makes:

> I'm really excited about learning to bind books in our class. . . . Whenever I get excited about something like the bookbinding project I feel like I could twirl around the room just like Cinderella or Sleeping Beauty. . . .
>
> I hope I don't fall into the trap so many new teachers fall into their first year, i.e., being bound to the teacher's manual. Am I just some idealistic student who thinks she's going to be the best and then sadly discovers that what she wants to be and what she is are not the same? So many students feel like they're going to

set the world on fire. But when they graduate, they never even make a spark. They fall into a rut and stay there. When my husband and I were in school as twenty-year-olds, we had such big plans for our futures. He was going to work for the State Department and I was going to work as an art historian at some museum. None of it materialized. We're just two regular people leading two ordinary lives.

As I re-read this I wonder what happened to the girl who felt like twirling around the room. Although I'm living an ordinary life, I really feel that there is something extraordinary about me even though I don't look it and maybe no one will ever know it but me. But I know it and I suppose that's all that matters.

Like Beth, Sharon's analysis of what she's learned in the class leads back to the first theme in her journal. She will be responsible for what she learns and applies in her classroom, and only she can travel that road:

[A] horrifying discovery occurred on March 1. On this day it was revealed that I could not possibly learn everything I needed to know about teaching Language Arts from one course. Although I am still somewhat shaken by this revelation, I will survive this minor crisis. Often I'm reminded of the time I learned to drive a stick shift. Many people had tried unsuccessfully to teach me but I never felt truly prepared for this challenge. One day, however, my boss decided that it was time for me to take the store's deliveries alone. He didn't ask if I was ready to meet this challenge. I suppose he just assumed that I was prepared since I had had sufficient instruction. He handed me the keys and an armload of medicine to deliver throughout the neighborhood. I couldn't tell him that I was too scared for this mission, so I bravely went. It wasn't until I sat behind the wheel, put the keys in the ignition, and sputtered out of the parking lot on my own that I successfully learned to drive a stick shift. I imagine that teaching will be much like this experience. If I sit and think, I will never feel truly prepared to teach. I guess that I will need to just jump in and try it. Only then will I learn to teach. I have also learned that I am the type of person who feels that everything I need to know I must learn in school. When I wanted to learn about art, I studied art history. When I wanted to learn about flower arranging, I took a flower-arranging course. When I wanted to learn about computers, I took seven computer courses. When I felt that I needed to know about parenting, I naturally took a parenting course. Much of what I learned, however, could have been learned equally well by engaging in some self-instruction via many of the books published on these topics.

Sharon realizes that no one will ever be able to fill her with all the information she needs. She must jump in to teach, and she will not reach all of her high ideals. But the person that she has not yet become seems to be learning to reconcile itself to the person she is now.

Making "Good Time" in Teaching

Sharon and Beth both spent much of the term circling around and back to a few key themes in their work. I also need to return to my original question. What does it mean to be a good teacher of writing methods students? What is the quality of my instruction? How do I know that Sharon and Beth have learned what they need to know to teach?

I don't know. I can't be sure. Perhaps it's time for methods instructors to write these words—for all our standards, outcomes, assessments, and evaluations, we really can't be sure of most of what our students know when they leave us.

But I do know that the quality of their writing in the course can't be separated from the quality of their experiences in taking the course. I know what Sharon and Beth have experienced—critical self-examination, wrestling to reconcile their beliefs with those of their peers, and especially, working harder than they ever have before to produce good writing. And in a writing methods course, I've come to believe this is what matters.

The free writing, choice, and wandering around themes were necessary for Sharon, Beth, and all my students to connect their lives and concerns now to their future as writing teachers. They also needed to develop internal standards for judging their work through these texts and experiences. This, in turn, can help them develop the internal standards they will need for judging their teaching one day.

Even when ancillary social and thinking skills development is recognized in looking at students, the quality of the writing produced remains an issue. If Beth's and Sharon's texts are taken out of the contexts in which they are written, objective measures like t-unit and inter-rater analyses can be used to determine quality. But those analyses limit our assessment of our students' place in a larger culture of teaching, schooling, and life that they will be a part of. And in this world, writing is a tool, not an end in itself.

Carrying this one step further, some, like Jane Addams (1902, 183), have argued that literacy instruction cannot be divorced from developing social awareness and responsibility:

> The democratic ideal demands of the school that it give the child's own experience a social value; that it shall teach him to direct his own activities and adjust them to those of other people's. . . . We are impatient with the schools which lay stress on reading and writing, suspecting them to rest upon the assumption that all knowledge and interest must be brought to children through the medium of books. Such an assumption fails to give the child any clue to the life about him or any power to usefully or intelligently connect himself with it.

Jane Addams is most famous not only for improving the quality of schools in the slums of Chicago but for improving the quality of life in those slums. The connections future teachers find between their lives and texts through writing is only the start of trying to deal with the many messy and challenging connections between lives and texts they will grapple with someday when their students write.

I reconnected with Beth after she finished my course to share parts of this text. She liked the epigraph of this chapter, from *Zen and the Art of Motorcycle Maintenance*. She then told me her favorite quote from that book. It comes early, when Pirsig (1974, 4–5) writes of making good time:

You see things on a motorcycle in a way that is completely different than any other. . . . You're completely in contact with it all. You're *in* the scene, not just watching it anymore, and the sense of presence is overwhelming. That concrete whizzing by five inches below your foot is the real thing, the same stuff you walk on, it's right there, so blurred you can't focus on it, yet you can put your foot down and touch it anytime, and the whole thing, the whole experience, is never removed from immediate consciousness. . . .

We want to make good time, but for us now this is measured with emphasis on "good" rather than "time," and when you make that shift in emphasis the whole approach changes. Twisting hilly roads are long in terms of seconds but are much more enjoyable on a cycle. . . . Roads free of drive-ins and billboards are better, roads where groves and meadows and orchards and lawns come almost to the shoulder, where kids wave to you when you ride by, where people look from their porches to see who it is, where when you stop to ask directions or information the answer tends to be longer than you want rather than short, where people ask where you're from and how long you've been riding.

I think all methods professors want to make "good time" in producing better writers and teachers. The difference in our instruction may be the difference in the stress on "good" or "time." That difference—stressing the quality of the learning or the quantity of ground covered—may change the whole instructional approach.

For me, it's a constant process of nudging and prodding students like Sharon and Beth to think, rethink, and think again about their personalities, knowledge base, and relationships with others as they write. And I hope this nudging and prodding will be mirrored one day in the way they work with their own students.

Five

But What About the Kid . . . ?

Their stories, yours, mine—it's what we all carry with us on this trip we take, and we owe it to each other to respect our stories and learn from them.

— Robert Coles, *The Call of Stories*

By now you're wondering about the kid. You know, the one . . . doesn't want to write . . . refuses to work in groups . . . disrupts most whole-class meetings . . . struggles every day to come up with a topic to write about.

Donald Graves (1989) says that every caring teacher has about three or four of these students each year. He speaks of a common experience for teachers:

> Often when you try to get to sleep at night, the image of one of them sits in the center of your forehead, applying pressure. Just when the image starts to fade, and you begin to drift off to sleep, another one of them pops into that space. The kids defy you to solve the enigmas they present. "If schools are for all children," they seem to say, "how can you make them work for us?"

I keep meeting "the kid." My students will soon be teachers, and potential problems are a source of great worry for them. But there aren't any easy answers for dealing with problem students. It's not like God sits upstairs with a cookie cutter, stamping out these students in uniform fashion. Each has a different problem, a different way of challenging the classroom norms.

I have my own examples of such kids. What about the student who never says anything during whole-class discussions? who is already cynical about teaching at age twenty? who never writes a full-page response to anything? who hands in a typed paper with fifty spelling errors?

"The kids" have the ability to disrupt the best-laid plans, to leave an entire class activity in ruins. At best, these students are baffling. Why aren't they enjoying writing and reading? Why don't they understand the requirements? At worst, they are horrifying. The first meeting can be like watching a cockroach walk across your kitchen table. All I want to do is get rid of it, get rid of them and the ways they challenge my classroom.

My class is, after all, my baby. It's my best shot, based upon everything I know of literacy theories, hours of marking overheads, and weeks of structuring groups and activities. I'd like to believe it's as close to perfect as a class can be. And then in come "the kids," the ones who gleefully pour water through all the cracks in this form I've shaped.

I've found two ways to deal with these students. Perhaps the most common among teachers, and the one I've resorted to myself, is to find a way to dismiss the challenges. There's a category for each student who defies. "He's just lazy," I decide. Or, "She's learning-disabled—the specialist will have to handle her." Or, "If she hasn't learned to work with others by now, she never will—she can write silently while others work in groups." We all have a personal language we can use to define inappropriate behavior. And textbooks, seminars, and classes give my students and me a professional language for describing those who don't fit our expectations. This language is power. But if we have the wrong attitude toward "the kids," the language also can be a weapon, as Robert Coles (1989, 18) writes:

> The story of some of us who become owners of a professional power and a professional vocabulary is the familiar one of moral thoughtlessness. We brandish our authority in a ceaseless effort to reassure ourselves about our importance, and we forget to look at our own warts and blemishes, so busy are we cataloguing those in others.

In this scheme of using our professional language as a weapon, the challengers to our creation go into their properly labeled box, and we remind them of the label if they begin to forget their place.

The other way to deal with the challenge of "the kids" is to meet it. I believe my students can teach me, and I learn more from some than from others. "The kids" have always been my greatest teachers. I will always carry with me Stephen, that budding engineer from my first college teaching experience.

My kids now, my older Stephens, have a keen sense of what doesn't work in class. And if I listen to them, the class can improve. But often the voices are still and small, for they are not accustomed to being listened to. I can spend a lot of time walking into walls, waking in the middle of the night, drifting off in the middle of conversations thinking about these kids, changing my mind again and again as I test out ways to work with them. "Yes, that's it—I must be firm." Or, "No, I could change that assignment." Or, "Hmm . . . maybe it's the structure of the room. If I move those tables forward . . ." and around and around and around it goes in my mind. Sometimes the smallest breakthrough with one student can be the biggest victory of the year.

Tammy

I recognized Tammy as one of "the kids" when I received her first set of journal entries. I read her words with a mixture of astonishment and anger. I'd never had a student who had managed to hit all my pet peeves about students' attitudes in five short journal entries. Tammy was negative about everything—peers, courses, teaching in general, the education major at this school in particular. I knew that Tammy was working many hours as a resident assistant in the dormitories and that as a senior she had a heavy course load. She was in a stressful situation, but so was I. If I could be positive, she could, too. My reply to those first entries was short and harsh:

Tammy:

First of all, I think you should re-read your journal before you read my response. Your journal is *so* negative. You manage to condemn all your classmates (unhelpful and rude), all your professors (tenured and lazy), your assignment (you hate journals), and the education major in general (basically worthless and not what you want to be doing). I feel like I'm walking across this landscape you've laid out of your life with these time bombs all over the place. Luckily, I've managed to walk through without losing an arm or a leg, but my feelings are pretty singed.

Your life is *your* life. I didn't tell you to take on that job or this major. You have made choices. If you've changed your mind and don't want to teach, perhaps you should change your major. It's no disgrace. I know I had to change careers a few times before I found my niche. And if I get crowded out of this space I've created for myself, I know I can go out and find another satisfying career. But if you hate a big portion of your life and are constantly stressed, no one is responsible for that but *you*. You've put yourself into this situation. Now it may be time for you to find a way to work yourself out of it. . . .

I think you may be hard on others right now because you are being so hard on yourself. You expect more from yourself than there are hours in the day. But your attitude has got to change if you are going to get anything out of this class. Your refusal to allow any of your work to be published is an expression of that attitude. This isn't my class or your class—it is *our* class. How is anyone going to come to understand your views if you don't share them? How will others have the courage to put their views, their writing, on the line in class if students like you don't respect them? Our class will only work to the extent that it becomes a community of learners. You're making my job that much harder.

You have challenged me with your words. I hope I have challenged you with mine.

I thought this was a fine reply to this student whose face I couldn't yet even recognize in the class. The writer in me even admired those sharp final phrases. There was some crisp, good writing in those thoughts.

But there was even more good writing in Tammy's ten-page reply, written in one sitting. I learned many things about Tammy by challenging her, and she learned much about herself by giving me an honest response:

After reading your [response] today my honest first reaction was "Go to hell." I felt like once again someone had asked me for my reactions/feelings etc. and I was being condemned for them. You see, I had the same experience with a professor last semester, and after he "promised" that everyone in his class would get an A or a B I got a C– and his response to me was that my attitude was not appropriate for my position at this university, both in the College of Education and in the Residence Life department. I know I sound like I'm sore over a C, but what I'm sore at is that a professor who asked for feelings and opinions condemned or said my feelings/opinions were wrong. I ask—how can feelings/opinions be wrong? . . .

Teaching has been my lifelong desire. My job is one that few understand. I could write for hours—but I'll give you the shortened version. My job is stressful. Any live-in position ends up being a twenty-four-hours-a-day, seven-days-a-week job. Right now is the most stressful time because I'm constantly given paperwork and deadlines—but I also have schoolwork! To be honest with you, I have no time for myself. . . . I know you say, why don't you quit your job? I really can't stand that attitude in people (I'm not saying you have it, but some people do). I *love my job*! It's the most rewarding thing I've ever done. I've dealt with everything from suicides to deaths of boyfriends to sexual assaults to discipline for breaking the alcohol policy . . . and the list goes on. Everyone I've touched means something to me and this job is more than money. The money isn't bad at all. It's paying my way through college—and that's something I wanted to give back to my parents for everything given to me. However, I don't feel like my job is too much. It takes up a lot of my time, but I would never give it up. . . .

I don't ask for sympathy—but I do ask a few things. Please understand that it hurts as well as angers me that I am asked to reflect on my life and my future as a teacher and then you react in the way that you do. I think . . . you came across my journal which was my honest feelings and frustrations, and you got defensive and took it out on me. I would appreciate it if you would allow me to share my feelings without being judged or told that I'm wrong. I know I'm stressed and I know how I deal with it—you don't. I am the type of person that holds things in, and however wrong that may be, that's how I react. My journal was my way of sharing frustrations I've been having. Also—don't feel like you have to solve my problems—but I don't understand why you had to react to that in the way you did—it is my life— and that's what I'm sharing—MY LIFE.

To conclude—I feel much better after venting. I was hurt and angry at your letter. . . . I will not share personal feelings any longer in my journal—I will treat it more as a professional journal to avoid any further misunderstandings. If you would like to discuss my "attitude" further IN PERSON, I would be willing to do so.

I'd never had a student tell me to go to hell before. As I read further, I learned that Tammy's fiancé had been killed in a car crash just two months before the start of the semester. I had to think hard before I responded again to Tammy. I knew Tammy held many important lessons for me as a teacher, if I could just find them. This is how I replied to her next set of journals:

I'm so glad you took the time to respond so carefully and articulately to my first journal reaction. I think the biggest problem I had with your thinking wasn't the content as much as the generalities. I wasn't hurt by your comments about professors. But I challenged those views, and your view of students, because I thought you were lumping everyone together. That's a dangerous thing for a future teacher to do. As I explained on that Friday, it's a habit I find myself falling into. I can condemn a whole class as "paper shufflers," when only a few are bothering me. And sometimes that doesn't get at the real problem at all.

I know I would have responded differently if I had known some of your "real reasons" for what you're going through. Again and again, I learn that students of any age make sense. Their reactions are based on a history. Even when I don't understand, there is a logic beneath their actions. No feeling or opinion is wrong—but I'll challenge it if I believe the thinking beneath it is too easy. And generalities can often point to little thinking girding the point being made.

Someone like you has it stacked against you—there is only so much time you can put into a course like this with your workload. That's why it's important for you to know I'm not going to arbitrarily hand out Cs to students I challenge. So don't feel like you have to be nice to me and act like you enjoy parts of the class you loathe. Sometimes my students' honesty hurts—but it's the only means I have for making the class better. You, I, and the rest are the only ones there when I teach.

Tammy taught me that "the kids" do make sense. There are reasons for what they do, reasons that are often beyond my classroom door. I can't expect them to check those concerns at the door, especially if I want them to see their lives as texts and their texts as lives. I had to work harder to put myself in my students' shoes as I wrote responses to their words.

Tammy also taught me some of the differences between written and oral communication. When I meet students with negative attitudes now in the journals, I will call them in for a conference to talk about what's bothering them. Putting my response in writing can create barriers, and I can't be there to get their immediate reaction. Now when I have a harsh response to student work, I always try to decide whether a conference would be less threatening to the student than a written response. It took Tammy and me weeks of compromises and tentative steps before we stood on solid ground in our relationship.

Allison Meets Rachel

While someone like Tammy can take up a great part of my thoughts in the early weeks of the term, I also find I am in danger of dismissing some students' abilities for all the wrong reasons. My students too often see children who are almost forgotten in schools. These are "the kids" that haunt them as they begin to visit classrooms. Allison was visiting a first-grade classroom at a local school for another class, and Rachel became the focus of her thoughts for almost a month. Her piece about Rachel went through a few drafts in workshop.

My Name Is Rachel

The tone of voice in which the words were spoken, rather than the words themselves, was what pulled my head up and around. The voice I had automatically registered as I was sitting with my back to the class, filling out my evaluation forms, was that of my cooperating teacher Mrs. W. It was the manner in which she was speaking that caught my attention.

"Rachel, what are you doing up out of your seat? Sit down! No, put both feet under the desk and don't get up again unless you're given permission." The voice I heard was not one that brought to mind the image of a nurturing, patient, or even concerned first-grade teacher. The words also were a clue that something out of the ordinary was going on. They didn't ask the student to recall what work she was supposed to be engaged in. They didn't even ask, demand, or tell the student to return to any task at all except to sit quietly and stay out of trouble.

I frowned in confusion as I watched the new child's bowed head swivel in the direction of her teacher's now turned back. Five seconds later she was sitting mindlessly playing with her pencil, which lay in apparent ignorance of its proper purpose.

I couldn't understand why Mrs. W's voice held that weary, irritated note in it. The tone said that any time spent with this student was wasted and unimportant. There had been no compassion for a first grader still new to the immense establishment and system called school. There had been no attempt to direct the student back to work on her unfinished handwriting paper, only a concern that the child not disturb the other students that Mrs. W was trying to keep on task. I wandered over and smiled, glancing down at her ignored assignment to check her progress. Her only product for the morning were two clumsily printed letters. Why was this child different? Where was her share of instructional time being spent and why did her new teacher already sound so fed up when she spoke to her?

I found the answer through bits and pieces of conversation with another student's mother, the class aide, and Mrs. W herself. Their answer was that the child's name was Rachel. Rachel had performed poorly in a pre-first-class test for at-risk children. Rachel had been dumped on an obviously unwilling teacher. Rachel is a disruptive influence in class.

My answer in return is that Rachel is an overweight, bullying little black girl whose classmates follow the example their teacher sets by alternately ignoring and belittling her. Rachel is only an eight-year-old, but one who has already learned that she invokes two responses from most adults, either irritation or indifference. Rachel is a child who is much too young to have everyone give up on her and abandon her to a system that is already attempting to hide her away in the classroom. Rachel is an example of a stereotype that is found all too often in our schools today.

After working with Rachel for six weeks, I realize that an attitude such as the one that the authority figures in her classroom display towards her is not a difficult one to cultivate. To put it bluntly, she can be obnoxious. She does bully other students without provocation. She can be lazy. She understands the role she has been assigned in the classroom and plays that part to the hilt, complete with tears on command, demands for constant attention, and a repeated pathetic cry of, "I don't know. I can't do it like the other kids."

She is in short an infuriating distracting influence in class. Yet none of this makes the attitudes she encounters either acceptable or deserved. It's all the more pitiful that she accepts her label and continues on a track that her behavioral stereotype has laid ahead of her.

Much too often there is no attempt to reach, let alone teach, children like Rachel. These are the children who are "dealt with." As long as they are rarely seen and preferably never heard, all is well and they are left to their own devices in an ironic semblance of peace. This peace may be easier for teachers and administrators, but is it right? How much serenity is there in the knowledge that there are seven- and eight-year-olds that the system is already failing?

The first problem with the school's failure is that it is a self-perpetuating cycle. The behaviorally diagnosed problem children are rarely given anything constructive to do with their time. They are generally given busy work which would make even the ideal student restless and dissatisfied. Unfortunately, this dissatisfaction leads to more of the same behavioral problems for which their labels were applied. These problems are products of their efforts to relieve the restlessness caused by the teacher's solution to those same initial behavioral problems.

The second dismaying outcome of the breakdown in our educational system with these students is that the system itself often permanently turns these students into what they have been labeled as. Rachel, like others, digs in her heels at any suggestion that she could be like the other students, that she could do the work the other children do. You see, living up to her label is easier for Rachel, too.

As it exists now the system tells these kids that as long as they don't break any rules, they will be rewarded by being left alone. They will be pushed quietly through the grades in return for their obedience and their silence. Is it any wonder that some of these children will see nothing wrong with the government continuing this type of care for them so long as they play by the rules? Welfare in the schools or in the real world is no more an answer to their problems than corporal punishment is.

The answer to both these cracks in the school system is simply to teach them. Teach these kids what they can accomplish rather than what they can get by with doing. Teach them the most they can be rather than the least. Teach them self-respect rather than self-pity.

Whether or not Rachel will ever be able to understand the system enough to write something like this, I don't know, but I'd like to think that the feelings and the ability are there. They only need to be realized.

"My name is Rachel and I'm not stupid. I see the kids younger and smaller than me with books that I still can't pick up because it hurts too much to know that I can't read them. I'm smart enough to know that I may never be able to. I'm smart enough to know what those kids and the teachers, too, think and say about me. I know all the things that I'm not, but I know all the things that I could be, too. I know I haven't fought hard enough for the education which is my right, but why should I have to fight for what is my right? I know I've failed myself, but that the school has failed me also. All I want is some help. All I need is one person to believe in me, before I stop believing in myself. My name is Rachel, and I'm not stupid."

I loved the power in Allison's words, the strength of her belief in Rachel. She and I knew that if we ruled the world, things would be different. Allison was writing from a soap-box to herself, reminding us both that it's important never to give up on students. I wanted to believe that a part of that will come from seeing the way I worked to believe in all my students.

Daphne

I've finally learned that those who challenge me with questions about "the kids" aren't rejecting the theory and methods I'm presenting. They are often the ones who care the most, who really want their own Rachels to be seen and heard. I've learned to respect those who challenge me with their behavior.

All, perhaps, except Daphne. The color of Daphne's skin wasn't black, but it was tan, very tan. Someone who has a deep tan in the dead of February at our first class meeting of the semester must have a pretty easy life, I decided. I wasn't jealous of Daphne, just wary. Her sunny manner was almost giddy. I wondered if she would be a hard worker in the class.

I try not to make judgments about students early in the term. But no matter how hard I try, there always seem to be some neat compartments to shuttle students into early. My intuition about Daphne was confirmed when she asked for an extension when her first portfolio was due. Students *never* ask for extensions for the first assignment. With a giggle, she told me she had forgotten the assignment at her apartment. I coolly told her to turn it in by the next morning if she wanted to receive credit.

By the time I received the first set of papers from students, Daphne had already missed one class. I couldn't connect faces and names clearly for all students, but I recognized Daphne's paper right off the bat. It was late at night, and I was in a critical mood, ready to pounce on her words if the proofreading was sloppy. This is the piece that Daphne turned in.

A Revelation

Two cars collide at rapid speed. You hear it everyday on the news. People are constantly fighting for their lives. As you sit and listen, you wonder how families stay strong, how people survive with the chances stacked up against them. You never think that one day you would be watching the news and see a family member involved in such a tragic collision. Yet, it can happen. . . .

My sister, Donna, was in a severe car accident. She was flown by helicopter to the hospital where she had emergency surgery due to massive internal bleeding. With nine broken ribs, a cervical fractured neck, and a two-part laceration in her liver, Donna had a thirty percent chance of living. She survived the first surgery, only to be flown to another hospital to have a second emergency surgery. Her chances for survival did not improve. Miraculously, my sister survived the operation but was stationed in the Surgical Intensive Care unit for eight days to continue fighting for her life.

Sitting in the waiting room, many things went through my mind. I began to remember when I was in high school and Donna in college; how I tried to keep the distance between us. I resented, at times, the way I was always in her shadow, always one step behind.

Track season was always the hardest for me. My sister was a fantastic athlete in high school. She broke record after record, always giving her best. I, like my sister, was a good athlete. But I was always one step behind, never quite breaking her records. Then it came to my last season of track. My last attempt to show everyone that I could be better than her. But instead of giving this last chance everything with the determination and drive Donna had, I quit. It was an easy way out, a way of getting out of the shadow. It was just too much of a risk. What if I didn't break her record? I kept getting closer and closer to succeeding, but I knew deep down I could never win. So I quit, blaming it on an injury. I even convinced myself the injury was the real reason for not completing my track career.

Then there was school. Donna was an exceptional student. She maintained a 3.8 grade point average in high school. I was a gifted student, but I was threatened by the shadow. I never quite gave in to the shadow until I reached my senior year of high school. One semester of physics was required for graduation, and the second semester of physics was optional. I loved my teacher. Unfortunately, he had one flaw—great admiration and love for my sister. Donna's track picture even hung in his office. This physics teacher was also my sister's track coach. My problem was that I was not "gifted" in the study of physics. I found it highly challenging and difficult. Of course, instead of just seeing the situation for what it was, I blamed my struggle on my sister's memory. So when the time came for second-semester physics, I withdrew from the class. I didn't want the competition of my sister's great memory in this teacher's mind.

As I grew older, I decided to just bury the past and begin to have a friendship with my sister. I went to a different college than her, so the shadow was not as threatening. I decided to chalk up my high school days as years of bad luck in excelling in sports and academics. What I did not realize at this time was that my sister was trying all along to be my friend. Even though the past always lingered in my mind, my sister and I became friends. We built a terrific relationship with time on our side.

Then my sister was engaged, and she asked me to be her maid of honor. When she had the accident, my head did a full turn. My sister needed me, and I was not about to let her down this time like I let her down in the past. I sat by her bedside night and day, making sure she was not going to quit. I just sat there and hoped she had the same drive and determination that made her so successful in the past. The same drive and determination I felt so threatened by. And at that moment it occurred to me . . .

All those years I thought my sister was my enemy I was only lying to myself. I was my own enemy. I didn't have the same drive and determination of my sister because I didn't want the drive and determination. I could have been just as good, if I really wanted it. Instead, I just used my sister as an excuse to not work as hard as I should have. No one created this rivalry between my sister and me. Coaches, family members, and even my sister never made me feel there should have been a rivalry. I created it. My family and friends only wanted me to be happy.

At the hospital something extremely traumatic happened. Our priest went to my sister's bedside and gave her the Sacrament of the Anointing of the Sick. All that came to my mind was that my sister was dying. Death. I never thought it would enter my life so closely, so soon. I began to cry because I was losing the chance to return Donna's friendship. I was helpless and afraid. Reality began to sink in. My twenty-six-year-old sister was going to be taken from me. I didn't know if my family could take this. I just stood there feeling nothing, tears rolling from my eyes, not able to move. I looked at my parents and brothers for support. We reached out for each other and entered my sister's room.

Sitting next to my sister and watching her fighting for her life, I realized that she was my best friend. I needed her to stay alive. She always accepted me for what I was. She never said anything negative when I quit sports, academics, and other. She always supported me in my decisions. I needed to see her smile. I wanted to tell her that I was sorry. Sorry for creating her as an enemy in my mind. I wanted to tell her that I loved her. As tears rolled down my face, I began to have faith in my sister. All those years of success were not because my sister was a quitter. Her years of success were due to her drive and determination. My sister was not going to die, she was going to live. She still had the same drive and determination. At that exact moment, I have never felt so much love, respect, and admiration for one true survivor!

Two cars collide at rapid speed.

Daphne's sister did survive that accident against all odds. Daphne shared with me her sister's long and painful road to recovery the next time I saw her. Daphne was having trouble staying on top of her schoolwork because she chose to go home at least twice a week to help feed and bathe her sister, as well as assisting in rehabilitation exercises. "I wanted to write about my sister in that piece, but as I wrote, I realized I wanted to write about me," she told me in conference.

As Daphne talked to me, I saw that every revelation by a student can come back to reveal something about my teaching. I think I want to learn about their lives; my own beliefs end up revealed. Some of those revelations are hard to face. I don't know if I ever would have found out about Donna if

Daphne hadn't written about her in that first paper. I might have kept that awful, unfair first impression of Daphne as an unmotivated and carefree student through the whole semester.

Daphne showed me that there are all sorts of ways to dismiss students or limit the way I see them in my classroom. Every teacher carries stereotypes and prejudices with her into the classroom. It's easy for me to be on guard against limiting my view of someone like Rachel. Daphne made me realize that *all* students deserve more than easy categories, good or bad. The challenge is to see each student as unique and trust that every student will reveal abilities I can never anticipate at the start of the term. The key to seeing students grow, and myself grow with them, is to build a bridge of honest communication. There are many barriers between teachers and students that I have to try to break through all the time, barriers I rarely expect or predict.

And perhaps there is no breakthrough at all. I've learned as a teacher, and my students have learned as they meet kids like Rachel, that we can face insurmountable odds—students who have lived for too many years with taunts about the size of their nose or the color of their skin, students who have been shuttled too frequently among relatives who really didn't want them, students whose voices were silenced one too many times before they ever met me. Sometimes we fail. But in the process of trying to understand why kids are the way they are, I hope we become gentler teachers and more compassionate human beings.

Jane

A student I'll call Jane challenged me to fail her in the course. She skipped required days in the schools, turned in work late, avoided whole assignments. It was a battle of wills. I called her into my office time after time. I liked her. She liked me. She genuinely liked the class. Her excuses were lame, and she presented them as lame. Through it all, she insisted she wanted to teach.

The image of Jane appeared in my coffee one morning, like one of those cryptic messages coming up from the black surface of a child's eightball. It was late in the semester. I thought of Jane often, and finally that morning the solution came to me. Jane really didn't want to teach. If someone like me, someone who cared enough to keep trying to work with her, would judge her incompetent, she would be forced to drop out of the program. Before I finished my coffee, I called her and scheduled another conference.

I finally saw the problem. I wanted Jane to be responsible and make her own decisions, even if that meant deciding upon another career. She was overwhelmed by the possibility of diving into the uncertainty of a new career choice. If I would tell her she couldn't teach, she would believe it. I was refusing to follow the script.

I met with Jane that day. There was no question she would fail the class—she just wasn't getting the work done. She had missed more classes lately because of a mysterious stomach ailment. The doctor thought it might be an ulcer, she told me.

"I want you to know that you can still teach, but you have to want to teach. I think you have to search your heart and see if this is what you want. I can't decide that for you," I said.

Jane looked at me blankly. "I've never been more certain that teaching is right for me. I can't tell you how excited I am about my future." There was silence. We sat awkwardly together for a few more minutes in my small office. She left that day walking gingerly, holding her stomach. I haven't seen her since, and I don't know if she became a teacher.

Jane made me realize how difficult it is to know what you want when you're twenty years old. The full force of realizing the responsibility of teaching isn't something I can control or understand as it hits my students. In the end, I'm only a methods instructor. I couldn't cure an ulcer, provide a fine career alternative, or even assure Jane that somewhere down the road the problems would work themselves out. My last contact with her was a low mark on a grade tally sheet.

No, I can't honestly say I welcome "the kids" when I meet them each year, when I face down their challenges. I don't always know what to do, and sometimes memories of problem students mark the low points in my experience as a teacher. But I wouldn't trade one of them for three students who dutifully do everything as they are told. My classroom needs to change. My teaching needs to change. And "the kids" are never shy about walking through those holes between my theories and my practice.

Six

Some Notes on
Living in the Real World

It's a challenge to bring off a powerful effect, or to tell the truth about something. You don't do it from willpower, you do it from an abiding passion. . . . Caring passionately about something isn't against nature. It's what we're here to do.

— Annie Dillard, *The Writing Life*

Some time ago, I heard a colleague discussing student complaints. "I have students every term who tell me they're unhappy with the teacher they work with in their school internship. They think she's lazy, or too critical, or too hard on the students. And I know that teacher, and she is quite dreadful. I say, 'Good. Welcome to the real world. You will work with many teachers who are lazy, who are lousy writing teachers, who you don't enjoy having in the same building. That's life in schools. Get used to it.' " I didn't know how to respond to my colleague, so I quietly exited our discussion.

Later that same week, I was walking down the hall in a school I won't name, past the door of a fifth-grade teacher who will remain anonymous. The school has skylights that leak. I slipped and fell into one of the puddles in the hall. As I tried to get to my feet, I couldn't help but hear what this teacher had to say to her students. Her class was quiet, listening to her bellow. "You are all so stupid!" she yelled. "I've never worked with such a big bunch of babies in my life. You talk and talk but you say *nothing* because you *know nothing.* Shut up! Do you hear me? *Shut up!*" I wondered how it would be possible for these silent children to be any quieter than they were now. I knew from talking to other teachers at this school that these outbursts could be expected at least a few times a day from this teacher.

And then I realized that I was probably standing on the edge of this real world turf of which my colleague spoke. I could imagine that almost any aspiring teacher would not want to work in this woman's classroom. If they had any courage, they would probably talk to their professor and try to ensure that other students wouldn't be placed in this woman's classroom, either.

When it comes to education, I refuse to live in the real world I hear so much about. I find that phrase "real world" is always spoken with the same breath and energy used to justify inferior classroom practices. It's an easy way to refuse to deal with problems that need to be addressed, and our acceptance of this "real world" is why much of the general public feels justified in condemning educators.

I lose my mind when I walk by classrooms and hear teachers call their students stupid or scream at them to shut up. I go crazy. I feel like marching into those classrooms and making a citizen's arrest. Surely there have to be laws against such inhumane treatment of children. But it's hard to find those laws, and few of us are in positions where we can change the abusive practices in some classrooms.

I worry most about what we teach our students about school change and relationships with colleagues when we welcome them to the "real world," when we tell them to accept the mediocrity and abuse around them as they fashion their own classrooms. What I want my students to learn as developing writing teachers is that they have the ability to change and shape their professional world—not just their relationships with students, but also their relationships with colleagues.

I think students who complain about the poor teachers are asking for something beyond good classrooms to observe. They don't just want teachers who will give them prescriptions to cure the many ills in schools. They want mentors—a close relationship with teachers in the field and professors on campus.

I began this book with a dictionary definition of *method*—an almost clinical start to a messy personal journey of professional discovery. I want to close with a description of mentoring, which is my most important work as a teacher. If the Greek root of *method* is simple, meaning "journey," the etiology of *mentor* is much more complex. The root word means "to love, to remember, and to comment." Untangling the web of how my mentors love, remember and comment upon my work is a continuous process, and one I try to replicate with my students. I also look constantly for evidence of that loving, remembering, and commenting in my colleagues, so that I can learn from it.

I was reminded of this a few weeks ago, when I received a call from a professor at the University of Maine's English Department. The voice on my answering machine was formal and abrupt—I needed to call this colleague about one of my advisees, Melinda, as soon as possible. These are not the kind of phone calls you like to receive. I barely knew this advisee—she had only been assigned to me in the past month. But the phone call signaled problems.

When I reached the professor, he spoke in an awkward, halting voice, explaining the problem. "Melinda hasn't turned in her midterm yet, and it was due three days ago. I asked her about it, and she said she had it done in her room. I don't think that's the truth," he said "I know her mother died of cancer about a year ago, and her father is struggling. She did not tell me this, another student did. I shouldn't know this; but I do, and I'm worried about her. I don't care about the midterm—we can work that out. But I think she needs some help. Can you intervene?" I thanked him for calling and told him I would see what I could do.

Not knowing the student well, I pulled her file and began to sift through all the paper in it before calling her. It was thick with course extensions and letters from the dean during her family's trials. But what caught my eye was a handwritten notation from a new colleague who was her professor this semester in an education methods course. The student had missed two classes. The professor noted he had called her dorm room and discovered she was at soccer practice. He then went to the practice to talk to her about attending class. The note ended by explaining she was now attending class again and performing adequately

I teased my new colleague about his trip to the soccer field. He was a bit sheepish. "How else was I supposed to see her face-to-face? She wasn't coming to class," he explained. I told him I thought he had done the right thing.

These professors and this student are careful, private people, yet there is a dance going on here that needs to go on in universities. We're teachers, not therapists. But there's a lot of grit in this student's life right now, and we've got to help her find the means to deal with it. From the English professor nearing retirement who takes the time to pick up the phone and call a colleague he doesn't know, to a new professor who travels across campus to meet a student late in the day on a soccer field, there is a sense that our jobs go beyond the time we spend in college classrooms, because our students' lives extend far beyond a class period.

Our students' lives are often gritty—they are dealing with particles of irritation, large and small, that get in the way of their learning. Mentors do something miraculous—they find ways to help you rub up against the grit and either wash it away or build it over time into some pearl of insight about learning and teaching you can carry with you forever. They care passionately about what they do, and they expect the same from you. They expect to see powerful effects from their teaching in students.

My most important learning always can be traced back to some grit. I remind myself often that my career as a college teacher almost ended before it began. Two weeks into graduate studies at the University of New Hampshire, I was ready to quit. I was daunted by the road I saw ahead of learning to be a college professor. I made an appointment with my adviser, Donald Graves, and spent a whole morning rehearsing a calm and measured speech about how this wasn't working out and I'd be on my way thank you very much.

I sat down in his office. Two minutes into the conference, I burst into tears. I began to apologize profusely, insisting that I was usually much more professional than this. Don put up his hand to silence me. "Don't ever apologize for being human," he said quietly. And then he handed me a tissue and spent the next hour helping me figure out what I needed to do next.

I have held those words close ever since I heard them. Teachers and students should never have to apologize for being human. Teaching is a profession that breaks your heart. We need not apologize for getting discouraged, and we need to have mentors who will lift us up, helping us see beyond whatever is in our way at the moment. What Don taught me as a mentor is the importance of allowing students their humanity.

When I think of those moments that led me to who I am as a teacher, I become even more discouraged about the relentless drive toward standards and outcomes in literacy education. In my home state, the debate about preparing teachers has shifted from an attack on current methods to a debate about courses or skills. What the argument comes down to is this: Shouldn't prospective teachers be able to demonstrate competence in key areas without sitting through loads of boring education courses at the local university? There are statewide all-day meetings, bickering, revised lists of skills, and reams of reports devoted to the need to reform teacher preparation.

For me, a discussion about whether a prospective teacher needs a course in writing instruction or to catalogue experiences in a portfolio that demonstrate competence in teaching writing misses the point. What any prospective teacher needs is a contact point at the university before going into the contact zone of schools—someone who demonstrates through one-on-one time how relationships with students evolve.

What we may be left with in the end is a drive-through teacher preparation program. McLiteracy for the masses looks something like this—the state gives you a menu of fifteen items you need to be certified. It might include a strong dose of writing theory, a dash of multicultural awareness, a sprinkling of writing across the curriculum competence. Prospective teachers then go to their local college with eight skills in hand and pay for the university to provide the other seven.

Or better yet, you may be able to develop these skills in your own home. Why commute through rain or snow to your local university when another college is willing to beam the coursework into your home? One of my favorite television commercials shows a burly father reading a textbook as he rocks his child and a mom setting up a dinner tray in front of the television in preparation for her evening college course. It's easy! It's fun! It's cheap! You, too, can be a teacher!

The image is absurd, but it's no more absurd than the professor who dismisses a prospective teacher's complaints about inferior teaching in schools with a "welcome to the real world." These are critical, changing times for college professors, and our actions will determine the shape of our teaching in years to come. We will get what we deserve. If flip, dismissive comments are the extent of our mentoring of teachers, then we should be consigned to beaming our wisdom through television sets across countless dinner trays. If we take the time to call advisers, to travel to the soccer field, to offer tissues as we help students understand the grit, then we will have the relationships with students that signal the beginning of all fine teaching careers.

At our best, we mentor—we keep our students in mind, we nurture them, we choose our words carefully so that they carry those comments away in their hearts and minds from our classrooms to theirs. At our worst, we convey snippets of knowledge in teaspoon doses.

As Bill Ayers (1993, 88) writes,

> Curriculum is more than pieces of information, more than subject matter, more even than the disciplines. Curriculum is an ongoing engagement with the problem of determining what knowledge and experiences are the most worthwhile. With each person and with each situation, that problem takes on different shadings and meanings.

That is the real world I live in, the world I want to introduce my students to—idiosyncratic and awkward at times, but always a dance between the student, the teacher, and the curriculum. And if all this doesn't fit your concept of what a college teacher says and does, I make no apologies. Mentoring through these means has brought me to where I am, and will take my students to where I want them to go as writing teachers.

Postscript

Long Roads Redux

Into my office bounds my former methods student Janet Walker, just completing her first week of being a kindergarten teacher. It's late Wednesday afternoon, a crisp early September day. Janet is bubbling with enthusiasm as she collapses into a chair across from me, asking me about my teaching this semester and about my family. I ask her about her new first teaching job.

She requests curriculum development materials for kindergarten, talks about the wide range of abilities and experiences among her students and what a challenge planning is. And then she adds, "But I think I'm lucky. The first-grade teacher had to throw out most of what she planned to do with her students because they just weren't ready for her curriculum. She's discouraged because so many don't even know their whole alphabet yet!"

I know Janet well. As I look at her sitting there, I realize two requests are being made here. One is for curriculum planning materials—I think immediately of a book on my shelf with dense, detailed descriptions of integrated themes and step-by-step planning for kindergartners. It's a short distance to step over to the bookshelf and put that book in her hands.

But I'm hesitating at responding to the other, unspoken question. Janet wants to know how to do her job well enough to satisfy any other teacher who will see her students one day. No matter how rich the curriculum, no matter how detailed the plan, Janet will never be able to get her students to the point where they fit into some neat scheme of "what first graders should know." It's the most important thing I hope she's learned from working with me—students of all ages will develop at their own pace. We challenge, cajole, and agonize at times, but we can't control the pace of learning. And we will have many moments of doubts and defensiveness because of that. That's part of the long, tough road Janet faces, the journey I and other teachers will always be on.

And so I do what I often do when I don't know what exactly to say to make my point. I tell her a story, hoping my experience can connect in some way with hers. "I think I know exactly how you feel," I say. "Just a few minutes ago, I was in the photocopy room chatting with a friend who has a daughter, Nora, the same age as my daughter Deanna. They are both eighteen months old. My friend knows I teach the oral language development class. She mentioned that she took a few minutes this week to jot down all the words Nora knows. Nora has over two hundred words in her vocabulary. My friend wanted some help in analyzing Nora's language development."

"As I sat listening to her, my mind was reeling. How many words does Deanna know? Maybe six or eight. Was she behind? Had we made a mistake having home day care? Was there any way to catch her up? It was all I could do not to jump in the car and rush home with some flashcards for a drill."

"And then I looked down at what I was photocopying—an article for the first meeting of tonight's class on language development. It's all about how different children will learn to speak at different times, with widely varying degrees of word knowledge at different ages. I know this. I not only teach it, I *preach* it to students. But my head had to overrule my heart, because we all doubt at times in our daily lives what we know and what we teach."

Janet laughs, and I hope she understands. We continue to talk about different students in her class, what's reasonable to expect for children with specific strengths and experiences. We talk about what kinds of records might best chart where each student is on her or his own path and trajectory of learning.

We talk about the never-ending challenge of teaching—having the discipline to strive to do your best, but knowing in your heart it will never be quite enough.

In Barry Lopez's *Crow and Weasel* (1990, 48), Badger talks about the power of stories in people's lives:

> "Remember only this one thing," said Badger. "The stories people tell have a way of taking care of them. If stories come to you, care for them. And learn to give them away when they are needed. Sometimes a person needs a story more than food to stay alive. That is why we put these stories in each other's memory. This is how people care for themselves."

I tell so many stories in this book, and I hope I've told them in a way that honors the students and colleagues who have taught me and cared for me in these moments of learning. I worry that it's not enough, or the right mix. Are there enough failure stories? Does the theory shine through the practice? Do I convey how much I still want and need to learn about working with these men and women who will soon teach? I don't know. But the joy has been in the doing, not the done. I have delighted in the memories of these incidents and in reading drafts of this book to my students. The stories have been nourishment on tough days, bringing me back to some simple truths about teaching and learning that are almost buried at times in the daily practice of my job.

It's getting late. Janet is here to begin her first graduate course in literacy, the oral language class I will teach tonight. We know the conversation in our office will continue throughout the entire semester, with more conferences, extra readings, dialogues in journals. We gather up our tote bags of books and papers, and trudge upstairs to the classroom.

It's the same classroom we met in last year, when Janet was my writing methods student for the first time. A long road, a short distance back to that room. But tonight, something has changed. We are crossing that classroom threshold together.

References

Addams, Jane. 1902. *Democracy and Social Ethics*. New York: Macmillan.

Albee, Edward. 1960. *The Zoo Story, The Death of Bessie Smith and The Sandbox*. New York: Coward McCann.

Atwell, Nancie. 1987. *In the Middle: Writing, Reading and Learning with Adolescents*. Portsmouth, NH: Heinemann.

Ayers, William. 1993. *To Teach: The Journey of a Teacher*. New York: Teachers College Press.

Biedler, Peter. 1986. *Distinguished Teachers on Effective Teaching*. San Francisco: Jossey-Bass.

Burke, Carolyn. 1993. The Burke Reading Inventory. In *The Art of Classroom Inquiry*, ed. Ruth Hubbard and Brenda Power. Portsmouth, NH: Heinemann.

Calkins, Lucy. 1986. *The Art of Teaching Writing*. Portsmouth, NH: Heinemann.

Coles, Robert. 1989. *The Call of Stories*. Boston: Houghton Mifflin.

Countryman, Joan. 1992. *Writing to Learn Mathematics: Strategies That Work*. Portsmouth, NH: Heinemann.

Dillard, Annie. 1974. *Pilgrim at Tinker Creek*. New York: Harper and Row.

———. 1989. *The Writing Life*. New York: Harper and Row.

Fulghum, Robert. 1988. *All I Really Need to Know I Learned in Kindergarten*. New York: Ivy Books.

Gallagher, Tess. 1985. The Poem as Time Machine. In *Claims for Poetry*, ed. Donald Hall. Ann Arbor, MI: University of Michigan Press.

Goldberg, Natalie. 1986. *Writing Down the Bones*. Boston: Shambhala Publications.

Graves, Donald. 1989. Speech at Summer Writing Program. Durham, NH: University of New Hampshire, July.

Guterson, David. 1994. *Snow Falling on Cedars*. San Diego: Harcourt Brace.

Keyes, Daniel. 1966. *Flowers for Algernon*. New York: Harcourt, Brace, and World.

Lopez, Barry. 1990. *Crow and Weasel*. San Francisco: North Point Press.

Macrorie, Ken. 1980. *Searching Writing*. Rochelle Park, NJ: Hayden Book Co.

McBride, Mekeel. 1986. Remarks at Poetry Reading. Durham, NH: University of New Hampshire, September 19.

Moffatt, Michael. 1990. *Coming of Age in New Jersey: College and American Culture*. New Brunswick, NJ: Rutgers University Press.

Murray, Donald. 1982. *Learning by Teaching*. Portsmouth, NH: Boynton/Cook Publishers.

———. 1987. Personal Communication.

Nathan, Ruth. 1991. The Importance of Writing Yourself. In *Literacy in Process: The Heinemann Reader*, ed. Brenda Miller Power and Ruth Shagoury Hubbard. Portsmouth, NH: Heinemann.

Ohanian, Susan. 1991. The Tantalizing Vagueness of Teaching. In *Literacy in Process: The Heinemann Reader*, ed. Brenda Miller Power and Ruth Shagoury Hubbard. Portsmouth, NH: Heinemann.

Pirsig, Robert. 1974. *Zen and the Art of Motorcycle Maintenance*. New York: William Morrow.

Rief, Linda. 1992. *Seeking Diversity*. Portsmouth, NH: Heinemann.

Sizer, Ted. 1984. *Horace's Compromise*. Boston: Houghton Mifflin.

Steinbeck, John. 1971. *The Sea of Cortez*. Mamaroneck, NY: P. P. Appel. Original edition (with E. F. Ricketts) published in 1941 by William Heinemann Ltd.

Thoreau, Henry David. 1854. *Walden: or, Life in the Woods.* Boston: Ticknor and Fields.

Watts, Doyle. 1989. NCATE and Texas Eyeball to Eyeball: Who Will Blink? *Kappan* (December): 310–317.

Welty, Eudora. 1984. *One Writer's Beginnings.* Cambridge, MA: Harvard University Press.